MAKING THE INSIDE OF A SHEEP

My Life at Worthington Foods

By Allan R. Buller

TEACH Services, Inc.
P U B L I S H I N G
www.TEACHServices.com • (800) 367-1844

World rights reserved. This book or any portion thereof may not be copied or reproduced in any form or manner whatever, except as provided by law, without the written permission of the publisher, except by a reviewer who may quote brief passages in a review.

The author assumes full responsibility for the accuracy of all facts and quotations as cited in this book. The opinions expressed in this book are the author's personal views and interpretations, and do not necessarily reflect those of the publisher.

This book is provided with the understanding that the publisher is not engaged in giving spiritual, legal, medical, or other professional advice. If authoritative advice is needed, the reader should seek the counsel of a competent professional.

Copyright © 2017 Allan R. Buller
Copyright © 2017 TEACH Services, Inc.
ISBN-13: 978-1-4796-0771-6 (Paperback)
ISBN-13: 978-1-4796-0772-3 (ePub)
ISBN-13: 978-1-4796-0773-0 (Mobi)
Library of Congress Control Number: 2017902901

Published by

www.TEACHServices.com • (800) 367-1844

Table of Contents

My Introduction to Food and Nutrition 11

Stirrings at Worthington 15

What Brought Me to Worthington Foods 20

Beginning a Business on Our Own 27

Bob Boyer Arrives with a Totally New Concept . . 34

Entry Into the Frozen Foods Business 38

Opening Branch Warehouses 42

Heroic Rescue 46

Product Names and Related Issues 50

Important Technology 56

Some Interesting People and Events 59

A Fire at the Factory 67

Merger 71

Work Hard—Play Hard 76

Spin-Off from Miles 82

Stolen Attache Case 87

Sales Meetings 91

Unexpected Opportunities for Acquisitions . . . 97

Buller Hall 101

Quiz Time 103

A Solid Foundation 110

Allan R. Buller, December 2, 1917 – March 23, 2013

FOREWORD

Our lives may see many changes in direction before our careers are clearly established. Some see this as purely the result of fate over which we have no control. Others may see it as part of a divine plan that guides us step by step toward a life God has in mind for each of us. I leave it to the reader to decide which applies to my life.

I was born in Canada, the son of devoted Mennonite parents. The butchering of calves, hogs, and other farm animals was an annual event in which family members and neighbors often participated. We didn't know any vegetarians. It never occurred to us there were any, certainly not in our circle of acquaintances.

It seems incredible that out of that culture a person would spend a half-century or more with a company devoted to the production and marketing of vegetarian foods. But, it did happen. The purpose of this book is to share how it all came about.

The first significant change in my life came when my parents, with encouragement from other family members, decided to join a church of Seventh-day Adventists. It is not a requirement of the church to be vegetarian, but members are encouraged to follow a diet free from animal meats for reasons of health. Dairy products such as milk and cottage cheese along with eggs from chickens are considered acceptable. This is sometimes called a "lacto-ovo" vegetarian diet. I grew up with such a diet as our daily food. It does not mean our family never ate meat. Holidays, picnics, and other special occasions sometimes included turkey, chicken, or fish. My four years of military service offered little opportunity to follow a vegetarian diet. For most of my life, though, I have been a vegetarian.

Allan R. Buller, Author, 2013

The Three Presidents of Worthington Foods, Inc

James L. Hagle
Total Years of Service:
1941-1990

Photo courtesy of
Harding Heritage Foundation
of Worthington

Allan R. Buller
Total Years of Service:
1945-1999

Photo courtesy of the
Allan R. Buller family

Dale R. Twomley
Total Years of Service:
1983-1999

Used with permission.
©Lifetouch Inc.
Photography for a Lifetime

PROLOGUE

During my years with Worthington Foods I never really felt I should write a history of the company, or even considered myself qualified to do it. But as the years have passed I find myself with fewer former work associates and less opportunity to share memories.

Some have said, "We need a history of Worthington Foods, otherwise, we'll forget too many of the important things we, as former employees, want to remember and which other people also may want to know more about." So, with some uncertainties, I will try to answer the need.

First of all, let me say this book is not intended to be a biography or complete history. A better description might be that it is an anecdotal account of some of the important events that took place, and the people associated with those events from the time the company began as an experiment in a hospital kitchen to becoming a corporation with two factories and over 600 employees.

As an amateur author, I felt it would make reading more interesting if I focused on how other people and I were caught up in the risks and excitement of running a food manufacturing company.

Worthington Foods and its predecessor Special Foods had just three full-time presidents —James L. Hagle, Allan R. Buller, and Dale E. Twomley, in that order. I served the shortest term of the three, but for the longest period of employment, from 1945 to 1999, and was the only one to serve in every corporate officer position from secretary to board chairman.

I have tried to cover at least some of the valuable contributions each of these men provided in the founding, in the growth, and in the impact which the company has made in the field of nutrition, and more particularly in the field of vegetable protein foods.

With few exceptions, all characters in this book are identified by their real names.

The only exceptions I made were where the events in which they were involved could be seen as reflecting negatively on their reputations. Where people are quoted, I have tried to repeat the messages conveyed rather than try to repeat the exact words used.

ACKNOWLEDGEMENTS

Evelyn Wiesner, B.L. Knecht, and Nancy Remer read a draft of this book and provided additions and corrections. Beth Mitchell provided reminiscences of work experiences at Worthington Foods. Thanks to each of them for their thoughtful contributions.

Spectrum magazine kindly consented to use of material from an interview published in the Summer 2009 issue (Vol. 37, Issue 3).

Mickey Buller, my wife and lifetime partner, has offered me support, encouragement, and love for more than 70 years. I dedicate this book to her.

Chapter 1

MY INTRODUCTION TO FOOD AND NUTRITION

I stirred sleepily as the alarm began to ring. The alarm persisted. It was five-thirty in the morning. Slowly a vague sense of responsibility began to penetrate my mind, but what? Then it hit me full force. *This is the morning I report to Doctor John Harvey Kellogg in the kitchen, to assist him in his search for a way to make an acidophilus milk using only ingredients from non-animal sources.* But how can an 18-year-old boy help in a search for a product about which he knows absolutely nothing, and in a kitchen of all places? I'll get the answers to these questions later.

In the meantime, I remind myself that I am at the Miami-Battle Creek Sanitarium, Miami Springs, Florida. The year is 1935. And, yes, I am scheduled to be in the kitchen at 6:30 where shortly I'll learn why.

Dr. Kellogg is remembered as a world-renowned physician of the 19th century. A graduate of the University of Michigan School of Medicine, he not only pioneered a number of practices in the field of medicine, but he was also an inventor of sorts and had gained reputation as an authority on diet and nutrition.

A number of the medical devices he invented were introduced into use at his popular Miami-Battle Creek Sanitarium patronized by famous people from around the world, one of whom was George Bernard Shaw, of literary fame, who had become a personal friend as well as a patient of Dr. Kellogg. Both he and Dr. Kellogg were strict vegetarians.

He made a visit to see Dr. Kellogg while I was employed at the Sanitarium as a bellhop. It was my duty to carry his luggage and see that he got settled comfortably in a guest room. In the days that followed I would see more of him as he and Dr. Kellogg shared their visit in the "solarium," a screened area on the sanitarium property used for sunbathing.

Another of my duties as bellhop was to see they had plenty of orange juice to quench their thirst as they tanned and visited. Because I didn't want to cause any embarrassment, I was always hesitant to enter their presence as they reclined stark naked on their cots.

Rattling the ice cubes in their beverages seemed like a way to announce my arrival, but I always found them so engaged in animated conversation that this precaution was unnecessary.

As the chief medical officer at Miami-Battle Creek, Dr. Kellogg made it a practice to present weekly lectures to all the sanitarium patients. These lectures were devoted to health topics in general, but more often than not became directed to diet and nutrition.

Among other points, he emphasized the importance of a thorough chewing of food, a habit he called "fletcherization," because it was a favorite subject of a man by the name of Fletcher who was a popular speaker on the lecture tour of that time.

Frequently Dr. Kellogg would devote his entire lecture to the value of fiber in the diet. He believed no food should remain in the body undigested for more than twenty-four hours and was certain an adequate amount of fiber in the diet would guarantee it. If a patient questioned how this could be assured, Dr. Kellogg would suggest the use of a "high" enema, the meaning of which I, as a healthy 18-year old, had little interest in exploring. Physicians on the staff were expected, of course, to encourage their patients to achieve a goal of prompt and complete digestion.

Dr. Kellogg relied on the use of a projector during his lectures. Projectors in those days were quite primitive compared to the computer driven visual aids used today. My job was to operate it. Sometimes it required shaking or reversing to get performance.

Now back to the kitchen where I am to help Dr. Kellogg in his search for a way to make an acidophilus milk with ingredients from non-animal sources. The sanitarium chef had cooked some soybeans overnight, and it was my job to turn the crank of an old-fashioned meat grinder to obtain the liquid he wanted for his tests.

Standing in his customary white suit near the grinder with a spoon in hand, he caught a little of the liquid he wanted for his acidophilus culture. As he ran the mixture over his tongue in a way similar to that followed by California wine testers in checking their products, his goatee would twitch reflecting the degree of his approval or disapproval of the sample he was testing. If he wanted more soybean milk, he would say, "Boy, give that crank another turn."

He knew my name of course, but I was always "Boy" to him including those times when I took orange juice to him in the solarium or performed other little jobs for him.

Ultimately, he was successful in discovering the right combination of ingredients to make an acidophilus soymilk—a goal he had been intent on pursuing for several weeks.

The early morning episodes of soybean grinding continued for some weeks often followed by Dr. Kellogg enjoying his favorite exercise—riding his bicycle. He would do this dressed in his customary white suit along with a tie and a straw hat. He presented quite a commanding appearance as he sat, goatee and all, very erect and dignified, cruising the streets, sometimes with one of his staff following behind in an auto to make sure he didn't violate any traffic laws and that everyone else on the street was safe. He became a familiar sight to everyone in Miami Springs, Florida and often

> *He presented quite a commanding appearance as he sat, goatee and all, very erect and dignified, cruising the streets, sometimes with one of his staff following behind in an auto to make sure he didn't violate any traffic laws and that everyone else on the street was safe.*

found his picture posted in the local newspaper.

It was my Sunday afternoon job to set up chairs in the parlor for Dr. Kellogg's evening lectures and later to run the "Stereopticon" machine, a noble predecessor to today's computerized projectors. Dr. Kellogg would stamp the floor with his cane when he was ready for the next slide to be shown. If he wanted to go back and repeat one it was, "Boy, would you go back one slide, please." It was inevitable, I suppose, that the information shared with patients in these lectures would penetrate my mind and get me to thinking about such things as the importance of fiber in the diet, the benefit of thoroughly chewing one's food, the impact of bacteria for good or bad on food digestion, and the value of fruits, grains, nuts, and vegetables in the daily diet. Dr. Kellogg was a committed vegetarian and in many ways was ahead of his time on what constitutes good nutrition. Perhaps this is what got me on the path that would ultimately take me to Worthington Foods, which became, in time, one of the largest manufacturers of vegetable protein foods in the world.

ARB (left) with older brother Lloyd Buller, while both were working at the Miami-Battle Creek Sanitarium circa 1935.

Chapter 2

STIRRINGS AT WORTHINGTON

While I was turning a meat grinder crank for Dr. Kellogg in Florida to provide an ingredient to be stirred into his experimental soy acidophilus mixture designed to help people maintain a proper level of friendly bacteria in their digestive systems, another stirring of ingredients had begun in Worthington, Ohio, a suburb of Columbus. Dr. George T. Harding III and Elwin Knecht, the chef of their health care institution along with Bill Robinson, a patient, were working together in the kitchen trying to put together a vegetarian steak-like food similar to one that Dr. Kellogg had invented and was producing at the Battle Creek Food Company. Bill had been a sales representative for the company and was familiar with the nature of its products and the success it had in marketing them.

Dr. Harding, as a graduate of the Seventh-day Adventist school of medicine in Loma Linda, California, was familiar with the dietary preferences of members of that faith. He and his chef, Knecht, had talked at various times about the need for a satisfactory meat alternative for employees and patients of their institution. From his experience at the Battle Creek Food Company, Bill knew that the basic ingredient for the food they had in mind was wheat gluten. After some trial and error samples prepared by Knecht and Robinson proved to be what they hoped for and "Choplets" were born, destined to become the "flagship" product of Special Foods and its successor, Worthington Foods.

However, Choplets weren't called by that name at the outset. The naming of the newborn product took place at a dinner held in the Harding home. Mrs. Harding had prepared a meal for the family and included some of the new vegetarian product that had been made and sent over by Elwin and Bill. The Harding's oldest son, George IV, about twelve years old at the time, was at the table. Everyone seemed pleased with the new product and conversation turned to the question of what name should be used to identify it. Names such as vegetable steaks, cutlets, and steaklets, were already in use by other manufacturers. It would only be confusing to customers if Special Foods used one of the same names.

After a number of suggestions had been made and bandied about without much interest, young George exclaimed, "How about calling them 'Choplets'?" The name struck everyone as being a good suggestion and should be adopted. In time the name became so well known that it fell into generic use as people made comparisons with what they referred to as Battle Creek "choplets" or Cedar Lake "choplets" or Loma Linda "choplets."

> "How about calling them 'Choplets'?"

The product rapidly became popular with employees and patients. Information about the new product spread to friends, who also wanted to try the product. Then people outside the local community heard about it, and demand for it began to build, soon outgrowing the space, time, and energy of Elwin Knecht and his staff. He, Dr. Harding, and Bill Robinson decided they needed a separate place to make the product and more people to help produce it.

An early label on Worthington Foods' popular product, "Choplets".
Photo courtesy of
Harding Heritage Foundation of Worthington.

Elwin had a brother by the name of Bernath J. Knecht,

a self-trained engineer with an entrepreneurial spirit. He was invited to join those already involved. A nearby house on Proprietor's Road—the same street on which the Harding home was located—became available and was purchased for $2,000. It was a humble beginning, but adequate as the first factory for making Choplets. The first floor served as office and administrative space; the basement was converted into the production area, and the second floor was used for storage of supplies. A new business had been launched!

It soon became clear that the new business needed experienced management. Bill Robinson said he might have an answer for that need. He had gone to school with James. L. Hagle who, upon graduation from college, had begun a career as credit manager for Hinsdale Hospital in Hinsdale, Illinois. Jim was invited to come to Worthington for a visit and an interview. He proved to be a good choice for the position that needed to be filled. He not only had business management experience, but he had also been a successful salesman earning his way through college.

Seeing potential for a challenging and promising new career, Jim joined the new company. One of his first proposals was to form a business partnership. After discussing the matter together, Jim and George proceeded with forming a partnership comprised of the two of them along with Dr. Warren Harding, brother of George, Dr. Harrison Evans, a brother-in-law, and Philip Hoffman, another brother-in-law. Jim was appointed general manager of the business. The partnership was still operating under the name "Special Foods" when I joined the company in 1945.

Very quickly Jim turned his attention to hiring more help to run the business. Luther Lyle, a former drug store clerk, joined the company as a production worker but was soon moved to bookkeeping. Bernath J. Knecht, popularly known as BJ, was already on the payroll and was shortly joined by W. Kenneth Case who had worked with Jim Hagle at Hinsdale Hospital. Other new employees included Lois Lewis and her father, Bill Lewis, who like Bernath, wore more than one hat working at various jobs as needed.

If small, successful, growing companies often find themselves short of capital to meet the needs of expansion or growth, then Special Foods was no exception. Jim confided to me later he often went to the post office on payday to see if the mail might contain some food orders with cash that could be used to help cover the payroll. On one occasion when the need was especially pressing he discovered the mail included a shoebox wrapped in brown paper. The box contained $5,000 mostly in $20 bills. There was no indication of insurance on the package, but the money was real enough.

The friend who had sent the money was Dr. Florence Keller, the mother of Dr. Frances Harding, who in turn, was the wife of Dr. Warren Harding, a partner in Special Foods as noted earlier. Dr. Keller's interest in the company went beyond her family relationship. She believed Special Foods had a promising future based on its commitment to producing vegetarian foods. From time to time, she would send money to help the struggling company. In return, Special Foods, and later Worthington Foods, would send her a promissory note for the amount of money she continued to forward from time to time.

Dr. Keller was a person with a strong personality. Stories of her experiences as a physician included a tale about her work as a 70-year old surgeon. In the operating room one day a resident physician made this observation: "Dr. Keller, I hope I will have a steady hand like yours when I'm seventy years old." Her reply was, "You won't. You don't have a steady hand now!"

Dr. George Harding III and Dr. Warren Harding were nephews of former President Warren G. Harding, who had been editor of the newspaper published in nearby Marion, Ohio. The Harding family had many physicians in its fold. George T. Harding I and his son Dr. George T. Harding II were key persons in the founding of what became, in time, the Harding Hospital for psychiatric care. Dr. George T. Harding III carried on the family tradition, and it was under his guidance that the hospital grew to become a nationally known health care facility with over 100 beds. By this time, George T. Harding IV had become an adult and qualified physician. He succeeded his father as medical director of Harding Hospital and would serve as a member of the Worthington Foods Board of Directors, beginning in 1981.

The employees of Special Foods in 1945.
Photo courtesy of Harding Heritage Foundation of Worthington.

Chapter 3

WHAT BROUGHT ME TO WORTHINGTON FOODS

During the school year 1940–1941, I was a student at Emmanuel Missionary College (now Andrews University). It was my senior year, and the other students and I who were expecting to graduate found it difficult to focus on career choices. War was imminent.

Europe was already embroiled in conflict, and our own government had adopted a military draft system. Draft provisions called for a year of basic training before a return to civilian life.

In anticipation of required military service for young males, our school had added a course to its class schedule offering training as medical aides. Those who enrolled became medical cadets and received formal training in the classroom and in the field. I was among those who joined and found the experience helpful after I was inducted into the U.S. Army.

During the school year Mildred (Mickey) Walberg, also a student, and I had become engaged. We planned to marry as soon as our financial situation and my military career made it possible. Army privates at that time received just $21.00 per month in pay, so marriage was not an immediate prospect. One of our teachers, wanting to be helpful, suggested getting married immediately might delay my induction into military service.

She and I discussed it as a possibility, but neither of us felt we wanted to get married with this as the deciding factor as to when our marriage should take place.

I was living at home at the time and attending school as a community resident offered some benefits, one of which was home-cooked food. A young man by the name of Bill Hamilton stopped at our house one day and showed my mother a can of "Choplets" made by Special Foods in Worthington, Ohio. Choplets soon became our family's favorite factory-made vegetarian food. I missed having them when I began life as a soldier.

Two weeks after graduation, I was inducted into military service and sent to Camp Grant in Illinois for basic training. After completing my basic training, I was assigned to duty in training recruits. I felt it would be well for me to provide the best service of which I was capable. In a short time, I earned promotion as a non-commissioned officer to corporal and then to sergeant. These promotions suggested I could now afford to get married. By postal mail I sent a set of my sergeant stripes to Mickey. She quickly got the message that I felt we could now get married. I arranged for a leave of absence, and we celebrated with a military wedding in Mickey's hometown, Holland, Michigan. We spent our honeymoon on an island in Gull Lake near Battle Creek, Michigan. She then joined me in Rockford, Illinois, near to the Camp Grant U.S. Army post.

Left to right: ARB with mother, Stella Loewen Buller, and siblings Verda, Bertha, and Lloyd circa 1934.

Allan with future wife Mickey Walberg circa 1941.

For many Americans the year 1941 will always be remembered as the year of Pearl Harbor. Those of us

For many Americans the year 1941 will always be remembered as the year of Pearl Harbor. already serving in military service knew this meant the end of our plans for just one year of basic training. After three years at Camp Grant where I helped in training army recruits, I was on a troop ship bound for Europe as medical supply sergeant for the U.S. Army 102nd General Hospital stationed in England.

US Army Corporal Buller reading his Bible in the barracks.

I was one member in an advance party of five with responsibility for obtaining from a nearby medical depot the equipment and supplies needed to have our hospital ready to accept patients within a month. Our manual of hospital supplies listed some 6,000 items from medical instruments to dental chairs, from hospital urinals to bandages, and from soap to medicines—anything and everything a physician or nurse might need in caring for patients. We held to our schedule and had the hospital prepared to admit patients for any kind of surgery, medical or dental, and any illness brought on by war, including the need for psychiatric care.

As an enlisted man with the rank of staff sergeant, I had eight men who reported to me, and I, in turn, reported to Captain Marvin Ware, our medical supply officer. The hospital facilities themselves consisted of a number of wards each in a separate building, with a total bed capacity of 1,400 patients.

We had a busy schedule, but at times unusual and interesting events provided subjects for good conversation and memories. Our hospital complex was housed in a number of single level buildings used for patient wards and for staff housing as well. Each ward was heated, when necessary, by a cast iron stove using charcoal as fuel.

One cold morning a male nurse arrived at the ward for psychiatric patients to help them prepare for the day's activities. He discovered that during the night someone had lifted the lid off the stove and used the stove as a toilet for a bowel movement. After the ward physician arrived and had seen the problem, he told the nurse he had an idea for discovering the guilty party. A traditional military practice calls for a periodic inspection of enlisted men to determine if any had become infected with a sexually transmitted disease and needed treatment. The physician announced there would be such an inspection on this day, and, in preparation for it, all patients must stand naked at the foot of their cots facing the center aisle. After performing a perfunctory inspection, he ordered all to turn about and face the outer wall. Sure enough, there was one patient who displayed a black, sooty ring on his buttocks. His punishment was to remove all ashes and waste and refill the stove with fresh fuel—a mild but appropriate sentence.

Mail call was a welcome break in the day's routine. One day there was a letter for me from Jim Hagle, a friend I had known at college. We both loved baseball and had played together many times. In his letter Jim explained he was currently the general manager of Special Foods in Worthington, Ohio, and asked if I had ever heard of the company and the products it made. I mentally responded, *Of course, I do. The company makes Choplets, my favorite vegetarian food.* Jim went on in his letter to ask if I would consider joining him at Special Foods when the war was over. In reply, I wrote that I could not provide an immediate answer because no one knew when the war would end.

In the meantime, GI gossip had coined the phrase, "Golden Gate in '48." It was about all I could say, or write, in response.

I didn't know my service as the supply sergeant for the 102nd General Hospital would end as abruptly as it

Allan and Mickey wrote to each other every day they were apart during his military service from 1941 to 1945.

then did. We received sudden orders to close down our hospital and were given one week to return all usable materials to the nearest army supply depot and all unusable materials to the reclamation center. Our commanding officer was also told our organization should be prepared to reorganize for duty in the Pacific Theater. All this seemed plausible enough. Military operations in Europe were beginning to wind down even though the war had not completely ended. The atom bomb was still just a concept, so the war was not over in the Pacific Theater.

Working night and day without stopping, we closed the 102nd in five days. One of the memorable events of the week had to do with what could be returned to the army supply depot and what was to go to the salvage center. We had hundreds of porcelain urinals, basins, and bedpans that were chipped. The supply depot would not accept the return of any items showing more than one chip of damage. Salvage would not accept any items unless they showed more than two chips of damage. We had many with just two chips of damage, so this forced us into a dilemma. What were we to do with those that had just two chips? This was Army bureaucracy at its worst.

There was an Army private first class from Brooklyn in our supply department. In an aside to me he said, "Don't worry about it, Sarge. I'll take care of it." Soon after, I saw him sitting on the floor with a hammer in hand banging one porcelain utensil after another being careful to apply blows only to those having just two chips of damage. I don't know from where he came but a British colonel suddenly appeared, and seeing our PFC on the floor happily whacking his way through a stack of porcelain ware, he addressed him in perfect Oxford English. "I say, young man, just what are you doing?"

The PFC's laconic reply, "I'm saving money for my country." Whereupon he returned to his banging, and the colonel left in somewhat of a huff while the rest of us tried to stifle our laughter.

Closing the hospital in five days also set some kind of record. The commanding officer of our hospital was Colonel Holmes. Through official channels he had received a verbal commendation for meritorious services. He invited me to his office. After I saluted, I heard these words:

"Sergeant, you have done a commendable job in the return of our equipment and supplies to the depot. I have just received word about how well organized the returns were handled, and the good condition in which everything appeared to be. Now, what can we do for you to show our gratitude?"

I was speechless. Conversations like this don't come often. Then a quick thought came to me, and I replied. "Thank you, Sir, would a promotion to master sergeant be possible? The Army Table of Organization calls for that rank for the position I have filled for the past year."

Then I trembled a little fearing I might have spoken too boldly. The Colonel's reply was warm and kind, "Yes, I know, but the problem has been that we already have two master sergeants in our cadre, but we'll see."

Paperwork in the US Army can move quickly at times. In forty-eight hours I had my master sergeant stripes and an increase in salary to $250 per month. Fewer than ten days later our entire hospital staff was on the Queen Mary bound for the U.S. on its maiden voyage as a troopship. There were approximately 15,000 soldiers on board. We slept in bunks built in tiers four high with each occupant taking his turn on deck for exercise and fresh air.

ARB's military service during World War II included responsibility first for supplying and later dismantling the 102nd US Army hospital near Salisbury, England.

We arrived at unloading docks in New York three days later to be greeted by hundreds of cheering Americans who had learned the first ship with soldiers returning from the battlefields was ready to dock.

After a short furlough, I was on a train headed for the West Coast where we were to regroup for transfer to the Pacific Theater. Mickey was able to follow close behind in a car with friends who were making a move to Oregon. Before our unit could begin regrouping, the war with Japan ended. We got caught up in the excitement, which filled the streets in wild celebration.

Our next stop was at Ft. Douglas near Salt Lake City where I waited my turn for an honorable discharge. Waiting was dull, but another letter from Jim Hagle arrived. He wrote, "Allan, don't accept any job offers until you've had a chance to visit us in Worthington."

A couple of weeks later Mickey and I did get to Worthington where I learned I could enroll at Ohio State University to pursue an MBA degree while working as an assistant to Jim at Special Foods. We met Dr. George T. Harding III, his wife Mary Virginia, and others while in Worthington.

Mickey and I left Worthington feeling it would be a good place to call home, following four plus years of life determined by military service and the uncertainties it entailed. We had very few material things, but we had each other and a baby on the way! Not only did I have a prospect for a job but also there was opportunity for graduate study as well. We invited Mickey's mother to live with us. She was single and had no other children. She spent the remaining thirty-seven years of her life as part of our family. In return we received excellent help in the care of the four children with whom we, in time, were blessed.

One of the first things Jim Hagle and I addressed when I joined him was to review the organizational structure of Special Foods. We concluded, after consideration of various factors, that the food company was now faced with an entirely new business climate. The war was over, and meat rationing was a thing of the past. From now on success or failure would depend on whether there was any continued consumer interest in the company's products, and in the ability of the company to adjust to the economic changes taking place. We decided operations as a corporation would place us in a stronger position than a partnership. For one thing, raising capital would be easier. After sharing the idea with all the partners, it was agreed to make that change, and with the help of legal counsel, Special Foods as a partnership became Worthington Foods, Inc.

Shortly in time after this, Dr. George T. Harding III was invited to become the president of the Loma Linda University Medical School—a position he was willing to accept if Jim Hagle would agree to become the business manager of Harding Hospital.

These changes were made, and I was asked to become secretary-treasurer and general manager of Worthington Foods. All of this had the effect of making my decision to join the company final and long-term.

Chapter 4

BEGINNING A BUSINESS ON OUR OWN

In 1945 when I began working at Special Foods, we had no employee with training or experience in chemistry or food technology. Fortunately, I remembered a former classmate, Warren "Kelly" Hartman, with whom I had attended Emmanuel Missionary College (Andrews University).

He had graduated a year ahead of me and went on to Michigan State University where he continued his studies and received a master's degree in biochemistry. He then went to work for the Department of Agriculture for the State of Michigan. His training and experience prepared him for understanding food processing methods, product formulations and the technology required to maintain pure food standards.

As soon as it became clear that my connection with Special Foods was going to be long term, I wrote to him to explain what we were trying to do and suggested he pay us a visit to explore possibilities of employment. We were pleased to get his reply indicating he felt he was ready for a change. His training plus his natural inventive mind made him an ideal person to manage the technical services we needed. He was placed in charge of quality control and product development. In time, he was able to make valuable

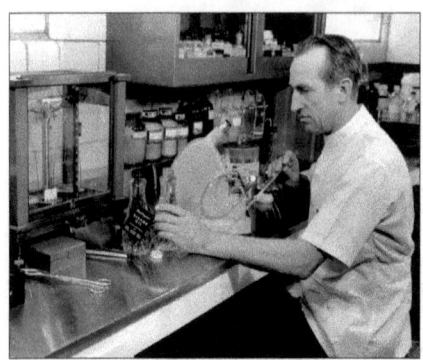

Warren "Kelly" Hartman, in the research and development lab at Worthington Foods (1957-1960).
Photo courtesy of Harding Heritage Foundation of Worthington.

contributions not only to the development of new products but also to the improved flavor and quality of all our products.

One day, after he had been with us for a few weeks, Kelly and I had a conversation about the importance of adding products to our line.

"So what do you think makes a product really appealing to the consumer?" I asked.

Kelly replied, "For one thing it's important that the food we eat is something we're expecting it to be like. Another way of saying it is, the food must offer organoleptic satisfaction."

Anticipating my next question he went on: "It must satisfy most or all of the senses we as humans use. If it doesn't do that, then we're not likely to feel positive toward it until we get accustomed to its newness, which may take a long time."

"OK, so a food must smell good, taste good, and look good. Anything else?"

"Texture or mouth feel," Kelly answered. "Flavor is important, but for some foods, texture might be the most important. If a food is not at all what we expect it to be, when we first sample it, we may not like it."

Joe Patrick on the production line at the Proprietors Road factory in Worthington, Ohio.

He went on to point out examples of foods that have distinctive textures, such as ice cream, popcorn, potato chips, various fruits, and vegetables as well as cooked dishes. After a little discussion, we agreed it is vitally important for a vegetarian alternate for meat to have a texture that closely resembles that of the meat it is designed to replace.

"This is the main reason" Kelly continued, "we find it so difficult to come up with a good alternate for beef or chicken. Wheat gluten does not have what it takes to provide the right texture. Until we find something that does, we will be limited in coming up with new products."

Kelly called me one day with a question. "How would you feel about adding a meatless hot dog to our line of foods?"

"Sounds like a great idea to me," I replied, "but I believe you said we were limited in what we can make because wheat gluten does not lend itself to the production of foods with a special texture, so how can we make meatless hot dogs?"

Kelly continued, "A couple of developments in food manufacturing have changed the picture for us. For one thing, egg whites are now available for use as a food ingredient.

"When added to an ingredient mix, the end product is firmer. Also, plastic casings are available. We don't have to rely on the traditional animal gut casings used by the meat industry. We'll have to get some kind of machine, or 'stuffer' to use in filling the casings. Maybe we can find a used one that will work?"

A few weeks later I visited Kelly at his lab. He showed me some open cans containing wieners that he had made. We sampled them. They didn't exactly have the flavor or texture of real beef frankfurters, but they were good! Because there was no meatless wiener on the market at that time, we had a strong incentive to move ahead as quickly as possible.

Shortly thereafter, we were able to buy a used stuffer for $200. It was scary to operate because it relied on compressed air to squeeze the wiener mix into casings held by hand on the nozzle provided for that purpose. Holding too tightly would blow the casing. Holding too loosely resulted in a limp product unable to retain shape during cooking which was the next step in processing. Relying on compressed air to operate the stuffer created potential for the stuffer lid to go wildly flying, causing possible

Relying on compressed air to operate the stuffer created potential for the stuffer lid to go wildly flying, causing possible injury or damage.

injury or damage. Careful operation was very important, and most employees wanted to avoid it.

Once the casings were filled, we still had to find a way to make the wieners the proper length. We found that this could be done by simply twisting the casings by hand to the desired length that would allow them to be placed into cans.

Cooking the wieners after they were packed in cans made them firm and guaranteed their shape. This posed no special problem for us because we cooked all our products after they were packed to provide desired firmness and sterilization.

The cooking was done in one of our conventional retorts which were simple iron cylinders serving as pressure cookers. Each held about a thousand cans per cooking cycle.

Packing the wieners in casings and using our customary method for cooking, required removal of the casing before the product could be eaten. We decided to leave this step for the customer to do—not a very considerate sales policy from a public relations point of view, but practical, and at this stage, quite necessary to make possible our moving ahead with plans for marketing.

Consumer demand for the new product became very strong immediately after it was introduced in our market, and soon we began to feel pressure for more production. We decided a night shift at the factory could be helpful, but it seemed like an extreme measure to answer a need that might prove to be temporary. Sensing the problem, our office staff responded by offering to help for a few hours each evening. Where, but in America, would you hear anything like that! Upon learning about the need for help, several spouses also volunteered to join the night crew. Excitement about our new product had become contagious!

For lack of a brand name on which our marketing committee could agree, we decided to identify the product for what it was—Meatless Wieners. This got us into trouble with the State of Pennsylvania's Department of Agriculture. It claimed our product did not comply with their sausage laws, which declare wieners must contain a specified minimum amount of meat. A quantity of our product had been seized and was being held as evidence of the violation, we were told, until we demonstrated our willingness to comply with regulations. In the meantime, further sale of meatless wieners in that state must be discontinued.

We had reached only a modest volume of sales in Pennsylvania and were willing to accept the ultimatum as final until we received a similar letter from the state of Michigan, where our sales had grown to a significant level. Because of that and the possibility that Kelly's former employment in the Michigan Department of Agriculture might be helpful, we decided to challenge the issue in that state.

After making inquiry as to proper procedure, we learned that our first contact would be with a justice of the peace in Battle Creek. We made an appointment and received a courteous reception. The JP assured us he was sympathetic to our position in the matter, but that his opinion would not really help us. He suggested we meet with an active circuit court judge and agreed to make an appointment for us.

With this much accomplished, Kelly and I began to plan for the presentation of our case. We visited a supermarket and picked up all of the food products we could find that were packed in a cylindrical form. This included candy, biscuit dough, cookie dough, and whatever else we could find. We took these with us along with copies of our product label, which clearly stated the product contained no meat.

We explained to the judge that in our view, a cylindrical shape alone did not call for the product to be called a sausage or wiener. We went on to explain that our meatless wieners were designed to meet the needs of vegetarians, and to avoid possible confusion on the part of the consumer, had clearly indicated on our product label that it contained no meat.

The judge was silent for a moment before saying, "I think you are totally correct, and in my opinion, are clearly free to continue making and selling your product. If the Department of Agriculture tries to stop you, I am willing to declare the Michigan sausage law unconstitutional."

For some reason or another, there was no representative from the Department of Agriculture present at this meeting. While we are uncertain as to why, we suspect it may have been prior knowledge of the judge's position in the matter, or of the position he would take if the matter ever came to his attention. In any event, this brought an end to our problem in Michigan, and Kelly and I returned to Worthington, feeling that justice finally had prevailed.

A new opportunity and a new issue came up when we got back to work. We discovered an advertisement in a magazine, featuring food-processing equipment. This advertisement described a new machine capable of linking wieners. We had been doing this by hand, twisting a long length of product into eight short lengths, which could then be fitted into a can for further processing. None of us saw any reason why it wouldn't do the same for us. As noted earlier, this still meant consumers had to remove the casing before eating the meatless wiener.

The machine we saw in the advertisement was modestly priced so we ordered one. When it arrived, everyone was eager to see it in action. We placed it on a work table where it appeared to be about the size of a standard typewriter of that era. It was scheduled for trial the next day, and I was eager, as anyone, to see it in operation.

When I went to the plant to witness its first trial, I was shocked to see it completely dismantled with working parts littering the workbench of our plant engineer.

"What's up, Bernie?" I asked nervously. "Why all the scattered parts of our new piece of equipment?"

"No problem," was his reply, "I just wanted to see how it was made."

Bernie Knecht, or BJ as he was known, was somewhat of a genius. He was also somewhat unpredictable. Although unschooled as an engineer, he was trained by experience. There was nothing he couldn't fix, or at least try to fix. His customary tools were a hammer, pliers, and screwdriver. There were times when I felt we couldn't have him as our plant engineer. But I also knew we couldn't manage without him. He lived in a house next door to the plant. This had its advantages. He made sure everything was working all the time. He had the new linking machine assembled and ready to try by afternoon. It worked like a charm, hooked in line with our stuffing machine. We all cheered.

But not all the problems had been resolved. Removing the casings before packing the links in cans for cooking called for a new way to cook the product to make sure the links were firm and held their shape.

Kelly and BJ worked together in designing and building an oven, which we christened, "the smokehouse," because it could be used to add a smoke flavor if desired. The oven was large enough to permit the entry of several racks of links looped on supporting rods.

Now we were prepared to stuff and form links, to cook them, and to remove the casings before packing them into cans. Because of the changes we had been successful in making, it was important to change the brand name as well. The new name selected was "Veja-Links." We applied for and received copyrights to the name. We also obtained a patent on the process for making them. The sale of Veja-Links soon exceeded the level we had reached with our former meatless wiener. We knew we had a winner when competition endeavored to imitate what we were doing.

> *The new name selected was "Veja-Links."*

Left to right: Reporter, Jim Hagle and ARB at R&D lab open house in Worthington in October 1964.
Photo courtesy of Harding Heritage Foundation of Worthington.

Chapter 5

BOB BOYER ARRIVES WITH A TOTALLY NEW CONCEPT

In our efforts to make products that could be used to replace conventional meat, we had discovered it is easier to duplicate the flavor of meat than it is to duplicate the texture of meat. As related earlier in this book, Kelly had confirmed this principle in some of his first experiments after joining our company. Appearance, aroma, and taste are important of course, but among the various sensory impressions received when we eat certain foods, texture can be the most important in the enjoyment of them. If they offer a familiar, or desirable, feeling in our mouths when we bite into them or chew them, it goes far in making a person want more. This is true for most meat products. Tender beef or chicken are examples. We needed that characteristic in making alternates for meat.

One of the basic ingredients we were using in making our meat alternatives was wheat gluten from flour, after washing away the starch. While it was satisfactory in its ability to absorb the desired flavoring, wheat gluten did not have the fiber-like texture found in most meats.

Our awareness of this problem and our concern about it had given us reason to search diligently for an answer. A surprise visit by a stranger in the mid-1950s provided an opportunity that was to have an important impact on the future of our business.

As I was scanning through some papers at my desk one day, my secretary Evelyn Wiesner called me on the intercom to tell me I had a visitor with no appointment.

The visitor introduced himself as Bob Boyer and apologized for not having made an appointment. He said he had been referred to us by the Corn Products Company and that he had something he wanted to show me.

After being ushered into my office, Mr. Boyer reached into his attaché case and withdrew several packages wrapped in foil. Upon opening one he showed me a sample of something that looked like chicken. A second package contained a sample resembling ham. A third sample, he went on to explain, was a simulated lamb chop. He said they were all meatless, and it was the reason he had come to us as recommended by the Corn Products Company.

My interest and attention were now fully aroused. I was particularly impressed with the texture I saw, and felt, in the samples that he placed in my hands. I quickly realized the samples had a texture that we had never been able to discover in our own production experience. The basic ingredient in his products, he said, was textured soy protein. This got more of my attention. Soy protein? That was a basic ingredient we were using in many of our products.

I began asking questions and learned Mr. Boyer had been employed by the Ford Motor Company in research during the years of World War II. His assignment was to find a way to replace the wool used in making seat covers for vehicles. The demands of wartime had taken all available wool for army uniforms and blankets.

In his search for a method to make a replacement for wool, Bob decided to try the technology that had made the production of nylon possible. In making nylon, a synthetic mixture is forced through spinnerets to produce filaments, which can then be converted into fabric.

A brief description of the nature and purpose of spinnerets may be of help in understanding the process. A spinneret is similar to the head of a water sprinkling can, in that it has many holes through which water, or other liquids, can be extruded.

A big difference is that spinnerets are made of platinum or gold rather than of tin or plastic.

Also instead of a few dozen holes in the head, there are thousands so tiny each is smaller than a human hair. As the solution used in making nylon is extruded it is formed into fine filaments resembling threads which when firmed and dried can be woven into fabric.

As Boyer began experimenting with the process, he discovered it was possible to use a spinneret through which a mixture containing soy protein could be extruded and formed into filaments that closely resembled the hair in sheep's wool. As the filaments came from the spinnerets, they were formed into a strand, which was then firmed or "fixed" by passing it through a special bath in which the pH was controlled. After drying it was ready to use in fabric.

At this stage in his experiments, Boyer was beginning to see success, only to have his hopes dashed when he discovered the filaments were not strong enough to make suitable fabric. Also by this time the war had ended, the Ford Motor Company was no longer concerned about replacing mohair, and Bob Boyer was out of a job.

Bob was out of a job, but not out of ideas. In reviewing his discoveries to this point, a new thought crossed his mind. If I can't make the outside of a sheep, maybe I can make the inside of one. The fibers are not firm enough to make wool. Maybe they can be used to make some kind of food like lamb chops or possibly chicken?

Bob then proceeded to try his new idea. It proved to be successful. In fact so successful he decided to apply for a patent that would enable him to offer a license to use his invention. With patent in hand, he set out to find someone who might be able to use his new creation.

If I can't make the outside of a sheep, maybe I can make the inside of one.

In calling on his first prospect, the successor to the Swift and Company meat packers, he found an interest and signed a license agreement with them. As time passed with no attempt, on their part, to use the license, Bob decided to look for another possible interest.

He was able to negotiate a release from the license agreement with the meat packing company and was free to search for another prospect. His new search led Bob to the Corn Products Company, which expressed interest but did not feel a license agreement was realistic for them. In response to an inquiry from Bob, Corn Products suggested he call on a small company near Columbus, Ohio, which was making vegetarian foods. He had never heard of Worthington Foods and didn't know how to contact us, but he finally located us and was making his call without an appointment.

I asked Bob if he believed his textured soy protein could serve as an ingredient in a frozen food, as well as in foods packed in cans, which we were already making. He said he believed there was every reason to think it would. I called Kelly on the phone and shared with him information about Bob and the purpose of his visit. Kelly's interest was positive and prompt. He agreed to see Bob at his laboratory as soon as Bob could get there.

During the years of World War II, a number of food manufacturers had begun experimenting with the packing and freezing of foods for public consumption. If the retail sale of frozen foods became popular, we wanted to be a part of it. We told Bob of our strong interest in his patent, and told him we would recommend to our board of directors that a license agreement was important. Our board went a step further and approved not only a license agreement but also an offer to hire Bob as a consultant if he was interested. This proved to be one of the most important decisions we made as a food company. It got us on the way to packing frozen foods as well as providing an important ingredient for the foods we were packing in cans.

WFI Board circa mid-1950s. Left to right: Kelly Hartman, ARB, George Harding III, Jim Hagle, Harrison Evans, Warren Harding II.

Photo courtesy of Harding Heritage Foundation of Worthington.

Chapter 6

ENTRY INTO THE FROZEN FOODS BUSINESS

	FROZEN FOODS WHOLESALE PRICE LIST — ORDER BLANK OCTOBER 15, 1963				
	Worthington Foods, Inc.				
		PHONE 885-5359			WORTHINGTON, OHIO
QUANTITY	FROZEN MINUTE ENTREES	MINIMUM PRICE	CASE PRICE	WEIGHT PER CASE	AMOUNT
	FRIED CHICKEN STYLE 24/6 oz.	.53	9.90	15 lbs.	
	FRIED CHICKEN STYLE 1/15 lb.		15.75	17 lbs.	
	WHITEMEAT STYLE 24/6 oz.	.53	9.90	15 lbs.	
	WHITEMEAT STYLE Sliced 20 lb.		21.00	22 lbs.	
	WHITEMEAT STYLE Rolls 4/8 lb.		32.00	34 lbs.	
	DICED CHICKEN STYLE 1/20 lb.		21.00	22 lbs.	
	BEEF STYLE Sliced 1/20 lb.		21.00	22 lbs.	
	BEEF STYLE Rolls 4/8 lb.		32.00	34 lbs.	
	DICED BEEF STYLE 1/20 lb.		21.00	22 lbs.	
	PRIME—Smoked & Chipped 24/4 oz.		9.60	7¼ lbs.	
	PRIME—Sliced Beef Style 12/8 oz.		6.90	8¼ lbs.	

When we began the production and marketing of frozen foods, we discovered problems that were new to us and for the most part not expected. During World II and the years immediately following, both military and non-military food manufacturers were doing a considerable amount of experimenting with the freezing of foods. Interest was focused on ways to improve the flavor, packaging, and preservation of foods.

The cultivation of "victory gardens," which had been encouraged to support the war efforts, led many families to try freezing of homegrown produce, rather than canning.

They discovered that freezing provided not only a means of preserving but also a way of maintaining freshness of flavor. The home freezing of fruits, vegetables, and juices became quite common. This practice had the effect of pushing consumers ahead of industry. Food manufacturers were eager to capitalize on this interest.

Freeze-drying of foods had been explored by the military as a means of improving the quality of food, and convenience in its use, but this technique involved the removal of moisture from products frozen and did not provide a satisfactory answer. We discovered, in our trials, that it created so much dehydration that food lost its appeal. Quick or "blast" freezing thus became the preferred processing method.

We were pleased to discover food in which textured soy protein was used as an ingredient responded well to blast freezing. What do we mean by "blast" freezing? For us, it meant quick-freezing at temperatures as low as minus forty degrees Fahrenheit with a continuous movement of air over products being frozen. A practical way to do this, we discovered, was to have a freezer room with at least 600 sq. ft. of floor space, providing enough room for several carts loaded with packaged products.

Two trained food technologists worked for us to assist Kelly. One of them was Dick Leiss, and the other was B.J. Porter. Dick was a graduate of Ohio State University and, as an active alumnus, maintained contact with the school. This provided opportunity to keep us current on food industry information, and to get help in solving problems as they might arise from time to time. B.J. Porter also was a food technician with training and experience. He joined us specifically to help develop frozen foods.

In a relatively short time, we had several frozen products all of which contained the textured soy protein ingredient which we had begun using after Bob Boyer joined us and shared his license and consulting help. Among these early products was White Chik for use in place of the white meat of chicken, and Wham, a product designed to be used as a vegetarian ham. These were followed by a roll resembling sausage and named Prosage to indicate it was a non-meat product containing protein with a sausage-like shape and flavor. Prosage Patties and Prosage Links quickly followed.

As the number of frozen food items in our product line grew, we were sobered by a problem for which we were not fully prepared. How could we bring these products to the attention of consumers? We couldn't afford to advertise because we used our money to develop them. We couldn't display them because very few stores, if any, had display cabinets. Those that did gave priority to stocking frozen vegetables and fruit, which many customers were already prepared to buy, because of their success in home freezing.

Keep in mind we are describing conditions as they existed immediately following the end of World War II. Our country was still in economic recovery mode. Most supermarkets, as modern as they might have been, were not yet prepared to offer frozen foods to customers. It took months before frozen food display cases became available.

Eventually, we had the opportunity to offer our frozen foods through public markets when Kroger's and a few other supermarket chains saw sales potential for vegetarian foods and made space available in their frozen food cabinets.

A strategic marketing move we made about this time was to provide a delivery van to our most productive wholesaler, J. C. Dimock, who had developed a substantial retail customer trade in an area centered in Maryland and extending to adjoining states. We purchased a truck with a custom van body capable of accommodating frozen or non-frozen foods and lettered with the words J C Dimock, with his address and identification as a wholesale distributor of Worthington Foods. When we delivered this to him and gave him the title to the vehicle he was so overwhelmed, he didn't believe we were serious.

In writing about Dimock, I want to add a note about his habit of calling me. When in need of merchandise, he usually called about daybreak and his first question was also habitual.

"Mr. Buller, did I get you up?"

After this had occurred a few times, I found a convenient way of responding. If the telephone rang in the morning, I would get up to answer it. Should Dimock ask if his call had gotten me up, I could say no because I was already on my feet and able to speak.

After products are frozen, they are ready for transfer to a customer's place of business or to storage. Food wholesalers prepared to distribute frozen foods to retailers were rare or too busy serving those stores already prepared to display frozen fruits and vegetables.

Finding a wholesaler who had the capability and was willing to serve our needs was difficult or impossible. In a matter of time, local delivery truck builders began to see the need facing frozen food manufacturers, and suitable truck bodies slowly became available.

As wholesalers of frozen foods were able to invest in trucks able to handle frozen foods they found trade with supermarkets more profitable than serving small health food stores. Again we were in a bind because of limited volume and by the restraints of our narrow market.

Initially, we solved this problem by insulating a section of our own delivery trucks and using dry ice for cooling one section. As marketing decisions called for opening branch warehouses, and we needed to get merchandise to them, we used the same method in our semi-trucks. Trailer manufacturers soon saw the market need and began making trailers with insulated bodies and cooled by freezer units.

Step by step we were forced by circumstances to solve problems in order to achieve our goals, but difficult as this was, the decision to move ahead with frozen food production and marketing proved to be providential. In a matter of just a few years, our sales of frozen foods far exceeded the sale of non-frozen products. Being in the frozen food business also prepared us for the later merger with Miles Laboratories, and in time, with the Kellogg Company, neither of which merger would have been feasible without this capability.

By 1986 we had outgrown plant production capacity at Worthington. It was impossible to enlarge our factory, because we were land-locked and blocked by zoning ordinances.

We decided to look for a second plant location somewhere in Ohio. After some searching and negotiation, we chose Zanesville as the site for a second plant. The city had invested in land to attract new business. We purchased twelve acres in its industrial park and became the first new manufacturing business Zanesville had seen in fourteen years. Some tax and utilities expense relief insured the selection of the site and purchase of the land. The new plant we constructed was designed for the manufacture of frozen food only. This information is included to further emphasize the importance to which frozen food manufacturing and marketing had become.

> *By 1986 we had outgrown plant production capacity at Worthington*

Chapter 7

OPENING BRANCH WAREHOUSES

By the mid-1950s, it was clear that our U.S. market was becoming geographically divided into three general areas—Eastern, Midwestern, and Western. One-third of our sales or more, were in the East, including Ohio, Kentucky, Tennessee, Georgia, and Florida. Another third of total sales went to customers in the Western states of California, Oregon, and Washington. Sales in the Midwest were growing but were still well behind the volumes in the other two regions.

It was our policy to pay shipping costs on orders of $100 or more. Because many of our customers were relatively small, we wanted to continue with this policy. The policy made it important to keep freight and other delivery expenses at the lowest level possible.

Because a major portion of shipping cost is related to the distance between shipping point and the location of a customer's place of business, it was clear to us a branch warehouse offered potential savings.

We decided to move ahead with this concept and began by buying land and constructing our first branch warehouse in Florida. The immediate benefits realized in operating our first one were so encouraging, that we purchased land and constructed a second one in Maryland. We added more but did so by renting space rather than building our own in order to conserve capital. The additional warehouses included one in Oregon, two in California, and a final one in Texas.

An important principle of management had been demonstrated during the struggles we went through in getting started in the frozen food business. It is not good management practice to surrender to obstacles. It's much better to be creative and find a way around them.

We were now faced with another big question. How do we get our merchandise to these warehouses, especially frozen products? Our first effort involved the use of rail service. It appeared convenient enough because we could load a freight car on the siding which ran along the east side of our factory property. But our first shipment by rail was a disaster.

The merchandise arrived at the destination with cases of food jumbled together and badly damaged from the jostling of rail cars while en route. It was also necessary to hire a driver with a truck to transport the merchandise from the rail car to the warehouse. Rail service was notably slow, and there was also the matter of how to keep the frozen foods cold during travel. Therefore, we sent our next shipment by common carrier truck, providing convenience and lower cost.

Our experiences with these early shipments convinced us that movement of goods by trucks must be our choice. Should we rely on common carriers, or would having our own truck be better? At this point in time, common carriers were not yet equipped to transport frozen foods. Having our own truck appeared to be the only answer. Can we make it successful? We felt we should get one and test the idea. If it doesn't prove to be practical or beneficial, we can sell it and rely entirely on common carriers.

Our decision to get our own truck seemed reasonable enough. There should be no problem, we thought. With some financial help from our bank, we were prepared to make a purchase of a tractor-trailer unit. Then we talked with a local dealer and purchased what he recommended. This proved to be a poor decision with poor results.

At the time, we had an employee who drove our local delivery van. We then assigned him the task of driving the new truck on its maiden trip to the warehouse in Portland. He called the next day.

His message was, "It's going to take me longer to get to Portland than we expected."

"Why?" was our immediate response.

"Because our new truck is having difficulty going upgrade in the mountains."

"What seems to be the problem?"

"Not enough power."

"What do you mean, not enough power?

"I have to use low gear in going up grades, and it slows me down to five miles per hour."

"Are other trucks and drivers having the same problem?"

"No, most of the other tractor-trailers seem to be doing at least thirty-five and pass me easily."

"Have you had a chance to see what make of truck they are?"

"Yes, they seem to be either Freightliners or Peterbilts."

"Well, let's discuss it more when you get back."

This was the beginning of a series of disappointments, embarrassment, and expense for which we were not, at the time, prepared. It was back to review and decision-making.

Another week went by before he was back. In the meantime, we did a little more research and discovered a Peterbilt or Freightliner with sleeper cab and trailer could cost a hundred thousand or more, not good news for a small company with limited dollars in the 1950s. We gave the matter further study and concluded we would need a more powerful truck. With a loan from our bank, we purchased our first Freightliner.

We also thought it was possible that we might need a new driver. Fortunately, it was not necessary for me to terminate his employment. He came to me and said he wanted to quit his job. After some discussion, I told him that if he wanted to quit, it was his choice and that he was free to do so if that's what he wanted. Shortly thereafter, we hired Jerry Stevens, a more experienced driver.

ARB with WFI truck outside Proprietors Road factory circa 1950.
Photo courtesy of Harding Heritage Foundation of Worthington.

Chapter 8

HEROIC RESCUE

Jerry Stevens was at the wheel of our Freightliner, when he and a companion driver, whom I shall refer to by the name of Otto, were on a return trip to Worthington. It was time for a driver change. They had agreed to make this change as soon as they crossed the Missouri River separating Omaha, Nebraska, and Council Bluffs, Iowa. Otto was already awake in anticipation of the change in drivers.

It was near midnight in late winter, and the river was running high with forbidding looking chunks of ice bumping each other on their way downstream. The bridge that spans the river at this point was known as the Aksarben Bridge (Nebraska spelled backwards).

As they pulled onto the bridge, Jerry rubbed his eyes. Was he getting sleepy or did he really see a young woman running toward them with shoes in hand? In a moment they passed her and Jerry realized he was not just sleepy.

"Hey, Otto! As soon as we get across the bridge, you take over driving, and I'll go back and see if I can help that woman. Looks to me like she's in trouble of some kind."

As soon as they reached the Council Bluffs side of the river,

Jerry jumped out and began running back to where he could still see the woman who had now stopped, and was beginning to climb one of the metal girder supports.

"Stop, can I help you?" He shouted.

"No! Just leave me alone." was the reply.

Jerry soon reached her and began climbing in pursuit. He caught up with her, and placed both his arms around her, tightly holding her against the steel support so she couldn't move.

"Just leave me alone!" she sobbed.

"Not until you tell me what the problem is."

The answer came slowly, but he finally understood. Her husband had left her and their children, and she felt that life had become hopeless. By this time vehicle traffic on the bridge had stopped and someone called the police. We learned later that no police had shown up because there were questions as to who had responsibility for dealing with problems on the bridge— Omaha police or police from Council Bluffs.

After what seemed like hours to Jerry, a fire truck came, and a ladder was extended up to where he was still holding the woman to keep her from jumping off the bridge. A fireman managed to get close to Jerry.

"How you doing, Buddy?" he asked.

Jerry's response, "OK, but I'm freezing."

"Just hang on; we'll have you both down in a few minutes."

By this time there were television and other news reporters on the scene. Jerry and the woman he had helped soon were in safe hands. Jerry and his driving partner made their way to a nearby restaurant, so that they could get some warmth and food. Upon entering the restaurant, they discovered a television was on, showing and reporting the rescue. Jerry saw himself, holding the woman between himself and a metal girder. Then he caught a glimpse of the chunks of ice, far below, in the river. Suddenly he was struck with fear.

After what seemed like hours to Jerry, a fire truck came, and a ladder was extended up to where he was still holding the woman to keep her from jumping off the bridge.

"Let's get out of here!" he said to his companion driver. "I'm beginning to feel sick!"

After answering a few additional questions posed by reporters, Jerry and his partner were in their truck and on the way once more to Worthington.

They arrived in Worthington during working hours, and I was able to meet and congratulate them for their heroic deed. I also made a point of relating their story to the Ohio Truckers Association, of which we were members at that time. Jerry was honored as Driver of the Month. The honor was repeated when he was later declared Driver of the Year.

Between the disappointing experience with our first cross country truck and the hiring of Jerry Stevens as a driver, we had acquired and used a variety of tractor-trailer units each of which seems to have provided a memory of one kind or another.

Late one night I had a telephone call from the drivers of one of these trucks. The driver making the call said they had stopped in a town somewhere in Kansas because of a severe thunderstorm. When I inquired if other trucks were moving on the highway, and if traffic overall looked normal, the answer was in the affirmative. I told him I felt this was pretty strong evidence that drivers, in general, didn't see the storm as too severe to continue driving, and that they also could feel safe in resuming their way. I was puzzled by the call until I remembered both drivers had been born near the coast in the state of Oregon and had grown up in an area where thunderstorms are rare

Every trip our trucks made to one of our warehouses meant we had to find a load of something to bring back. Finding return loads that were exempt from legal requirements was somewhat of a problem for us. Most of the time we were able to find products like hay or lumber available. For several years we shared office space with a lumber company, so it was mutually convenient for us to bring back a load now and then

On one return trip, we had a load of 2x4s. When the drivers stopped at a state operated weigh station, they learned they were overweight. The highway patrol officer on duty informed our drivers they could remove part of the load and store it on the grounds to be picked up the next time our truck went through the area. They took about 300 of the 2x4s and stacked them at the weigh station. On their next trip, they tried to pick them up only to find there was not one left. All the rest had disappeared.

The patrol officer on duty was not the same one who had been there when the lumber was left, so he could offer no help in locating the missing pieces.

Then there was the night I had a call from one of the two drivers, making a return trip to Worthington with a full load of hay. He told me there had been an accident. He then told me the story of what happened. As they were going down grade on a highway in a mountainous area out West, they suddenly came to a curve in the road, going too fast to make the turn. As they hit a ditch, the heavy trailer pushed the cab and engine of the tractor off the truck's frame, leaving the wheels still attached. Miraculously, neither driver was injured, the truck did not catch fire, and no other vehicle was involved. The truck was a total loss. Insurance covered all but $1,000 of the cost of replacement.

While I didn't get a lot of sleep that night, I still felt grateful, realizing the news could have been a lot worse.

Chapter 9

PRODUCT NAMES AND RELATED ISSUES

Sometimes we felt it was more difficult to come up with a name for a new product than to invent the product itself. Perhaps this is more of a tribute to Kelly's research and developmental skills than to the creative thinking of our marketing committee. The process of picking a name usually began when Kelly had a new product ready for taste, testing, and marketing evaluation. An example of the process is described in the following paragraph.

Shortly after we began making frozen foods, Kelly submitted a chicken-like product. It resembled cold cut chicken slices. We all agreed it looked and tasted much like it was designed to be, but what shall we call it? After some discussion we settled on the name "White Chik" and added a further descriptive word "slices." At first there was little enthusiasm for the name, but nothing better was proposed, so it was adopted. Later "White Chik Rolls" was added to the product line in response to the need for a size that could be used by schools, hospitals, and other institutions. Chefs could slice or dice it as they might

> *Sometimes we felt it was more difficult to come up with a name for a new product than to invent the product itself.*

choose. A small one-pound roll for home use was submitted for evaluation, and was quickly accepted as a "White Chik Chub."

Choosing and naming other chicken-like products was more difficult. Our marketing committee suggested a product that could be used in place of fried chicken, which might offer good sales potential. Kelly's experiments led to the development of a product that was intended to be a vegetarian chicken drumstick. For lack of a bone he used a wood tongue depressor. After much discussion in picking a name, we decided to go with "Fry Stick." The product had a very short life on the market. Whether it was the name we chose, or the product itself, we never learned.

A second product failure involved a canned vegetarian food. Had it resembled a meat product, we might have found more success in choosing a name for it. It was simply a sliced food packed with a gravy sauce. The taste was acceptable, but no one trying it could relate it to anything he or she had ever eaten. We asked Kelly what it was supposed to be.

He only shrugged his shoulders and said, "We called it Experiment Number 209 in our lab, but we didn't think it resembled any particular product."

Someone chuckled and said, "Maybe that's the name we should use." Looking back on the matter now, it seems like a stupid decision, but we finally settled on "209" as the name. A few customers ordered trial quantities. Six months later the item was dropped from our price lists and order blanks.

In contrast to the failure of "Fry Sticks," we had more success with "Chik Nuggets." They looked and tasted similar to real fried chicken pieces, so the product and name were more compatible.

People sometimes asked us why we didn't simply identify our products as artificial meat or meat substitutes. We chose not to use the terms "artificial" or "substitute," because they suggest some degree of inferiority. We believed this position had validity.

While we had no confirmation of it from any source, we felt that such well-known products as nylon and margarine were readily accepted with generic names. Had the producers chosen "artificial silk" or "butter substitute" as a way to position their products on the market, it seems doubtful they would have been as successful.

Our own product name "Choplets" was in danger of becoming generic when consumers frequently commented on Worthington

"Choplets," in comparing them with what they called Cedar Lake "choplets" when they really meant Cedar Lake "Chops," or in comparing them with Battle Creek "choplets," when they should have said Battle Creek Steaklets. After this was repeatedly brought to our attention, we decided to register the name as a trademark. It was our best selling product for many years; therefore, protecting the name "Choplets" was important.

In 1960 we wanted to add a caffeine-free tea to our product line. That same year, we acquired the business of the Battle Creek Food Company. All rights to use the names of products and registered trademarks were included in the purchase agreement. At the time, Battle Creek Foods had plans to offer a caffeine-free tea and had chosen the name "Minute Brew." We liked the name and decided to we could use it to identify our own tea sometime in the future.

We began looking for a way to import rooibos red tea from Africa. Our search was brought to a temporary halt by a telephone call. The caller said he was a representative of a well-known European beverage company and had just arrived in New York from Europe. He asked if a visit with me in Worthington would be possible while he was in America.

"Of course," I replied, wondering what the purpose of his visit might be.

He arrived the next day, and we began our visit. At first, there seemed to be a little tension in our conversation, but as we talked the atmosphere became more relaxed, and he soon seemed ready to explain the purpose of his visit. He said his company wanted to move ahead with plans for adding a product to their line, and had decided "Minute Brew" would be a good name to identify it. In responding, I pointed out it was a registered trademark, the full ownership of which we received at the time of our purchase of the Battle Creek Food Company. After pausing a moment, he said his company was now aware of our ownership of the trademark. Then he went on to ask if our company might consider selling its ownership rights. By this time, I had an impression that his company already had gone beyond interest in the name, possibly making some important commitments in preparation for marketing.

It gave me reason for a pause before responding, "This is a matter which our board of directors will have to consider. Our board will be meeting within two weeks. I will share the question with them."

The visitor thanked me, and after saying he would call by phone for an answer, he left.

When I presented the matter to our board, I was asked for a suggestion as to what action should be taken. I replied, "My recommendation is to sell the trademark for $50,000."

I went on to say, "We can find another name for our tea, and the money we receive can be used in preparing our own product for marketing."

I was surprised by the response of the board members. "Allan, your recommendation has merit, but the price you suggest seems a bit grandiose. We'll be lucky to get $25,000," and that's how the vote went. I was somewhat stunned. When I notified the representative of the beverage company of the board's decision and requested a check for $25,000, I detected a note of relief in his quick acceptance of the price suggested. For me, it simply confirmed the cliché, "You can't win them all."

So now we were ready to tackle the matter of our own plans for an herb tea. We found an acceptable arrangement for importing product and chose "Kaffir Tea" as a name for it.

A missionary friend who had spent time in Africa told us confidentially our choice of the word "Kaffir" was unfortunate because it was considered a pejorative term in Africa. We quickly chose "Kaffree" to replace "Kaffir." We felt this name added further emphasis to the absence of caffeine in the tea.

We were successful in marketing Kaffree Tea packed in jars, so we asked ourselves the question, "Why don't we package it in bags like regular tea is packaged and sold?" A little informal survey among our customers told us it was worth a trial. The biggest obstacle was finding packaging equipment suitable for what we believed would be a limited volume compared to the volumes packaged and sold by internationally known tea companies. A decision to move ahead with the plan proved to be fortunate. We found immediate acceptance of our new packaging.

Our success with Kaffree Tea also led us into thinking a caffeine-free coffee replacement should have good market appeal. In exploring potential help in supply and packaging, we turned to the same large European beverage company, which had found success in making a cereal-based coffee replacement and simply became another customer. We chose "Roma" as the name for this product, as suggested by Frank Poston, our advertising manager, who had a knack for developing product names as well as attractive packaging and labels.

Just as other food manufacturers have found by experience, Worthington Foods had almost as many new product failures as it had successes. In our case, most of the failures were due to a lack of market testing. Rather than spending money on market testing, we found it less costly to introduce a new product without it. Generally speaking, our costs in placing a new product on the market were limited to the expenses of research, containers, labels, and ingredients if the new product required ingredients not used in other products we were making. Having people on the payroll doing research and development, whether it resulted in a new product or not, was still a big expense.

> *Just as other food manufacturers have found by experience, Worthington Foods had almost as many new product failures as it had successes.*

Our advertising budget was very small—less than 5 percent of sales. Serving a specialty market was the main reason for this. Our customers did not expect a heavy investment in promotion. This is quite different from what is expected from companies selling products to supermarkets, where stores often will not stock a new item without some guarantee of promotion. When we approached large public markets in cities like New York, we found store managers often asking for significant payments of cash just to cover the stocking of shelves plus advertising to attract customers.

In searching for a way to reduce costs, we looked for a way to market one of our by-products. For years we depended upon using gluten from wheat flour after first washing away the starch. Because starch comprises most of the bulk in flour, the process represented a significant cost in waste. We began looking for a possible by-product made from starch. After some development effort, Kelly discovered we could make a liquid starch that was usable in the same way traditional cornstarch is used. We selected the name "Quid" for the bottled product, obviously taken from the word liquid. But it didn't sell. We couldn't even give it away—zero market! If we had been able to do a market test, we might have been able to avoid this experience. However, we continued to make and sell dried starch for wallpaper paste.

Chapter 10

IMPORTANT TECHNOLOGY

Left to right: Bernath ("Bernie" or "BJ") Knecht and unidentified man in the engine room, 1967.
Photo courtesy of Harding Heritage Foundation of Worthington.

If we wanted to maintain our goal of producing the best tasting, most nutritious, vegetarian meat alternate at the lowest possible cost, it was important for us to keep pace with developing technology. Fortunately, we had engineers on our staff who also saw the importance of this.

During the early 1960s, it was necessary to expand our research and development facilities as well as production space. Up to this time, we had depended mainly on the architectural services of Wellington Nicola, who was the son of a former administrator at Harding Hospital and a fellow member of the local Seventh-day Adventist Church.

Wellington worked closely with the Parker Garwick construction company, whose services we had frequently used in providing new buildings until Mr. Garwick died and his firm was dissolved.

Important Technology

We were unable to find a local builder who could replace the Garwick Company and looked elsewhere. We were able to locate a construction company in Cleveland by the name of Ferguson that had a good reputation and was qualified and interested in working with us on plans for further expansion.

We had been relying on the Ralston Company in St. Louis for our supplies of spun soy protein fiber being produced by that firm under the Boyer patent. Ralston was encouraging us to consider spinning fiber for our own needs since they had no other customers for the product. Also, we wanted to do this for our own convenience.

It was within this framework of planning and need that our own engineers initiated important action. The utility firm that had been providing us with electrical energy indicated an unwillingness to provide service for our proposed blast freezing and storage freezer space. Our engineers found a way to meet our needs with the installation of natural gas powered equipment, which worked fine. The electric utility company decided it could provide the increased service we needed.

Following the decision by the utility company to provide the service needed, our engineers rewired the entire manufacturing facility changing our requirements from 240 volts to 440 volts. This change lowered the cost of expanding the electrical system and made it practical to supply all of the buildings from one service.

In 1967 the general office building was doubled in size. A large 350-ton water chiller was installed to provide air conditioning for the plant, the research and development building, and the general office space. The chiller was a new design using male and female rotary helical screws to act as the compressor made by Dunham-Bush in West Hartford, Connecticut. The first machine received bore serial number 3, so this made us an early adopter of the system. Compressors of this type were simply called screw machines. By the early 1970s, Worthington Foods had the largest collection of screw machines in the world.

One of the bottlenecks in production was slicing loaves of product to make packages of sliced luncheon analogs. B.J. Knecht and B.L. Knecht, father and son, worked together as a team in designing and constructing a multiple-station slicing machine capable of cutting up to a thousand slices per minute and arranging them in a straight stack or shingled stack. A patent was applied for and granted.

The capability of freezing large volumes of luncheon slices created a great amount of pressure on cooling the stainless-steel molds that were used to shape and contain the product for cooking. Both round and square molds were used for various products.

We air-cooled the molds overnight, wherever there was space, but we soon ran out of territory for cooling the molds. B.L. came up with the idea of water-cooling the molds, which greatly increased the production rate. Then we discovered product contamination, with the cooling water as prime suspect as the source of contamination. B.L. corrected that by finding a method for air-cooling the molds. But to optimize the cooling and avoid freezing the product, it was necessary to determine the thermal conductivity of the various food products we were making. Because this was all new technology, no published tables with this information were available. He developed a test apparatus to measure thermal conductivity and showed a draftsman, whom we had recently hired, how to do graphical heat transfer analysis. This provided a temperature profile needed to keep the skin of the product at the freezing point without actually freezing it. The next step was to devise a variable temperature refrigeration system. This necessitated the purchase of a second screw machine condensing unit for the mold cooling system.

Most of the buildings at our Worthington plant site were one-story, and a multi-floor factory was really needed. This is when the H.K. Ferguson Company, located in Cleveland, Ohio, entered the picture. The need for capital to build a new plant became an important factor in the decision to consider a merger with Miles Laboratories. The merger took place in 1970. Miles agreed a new factory was needed and gave its approval to what was being planned. The house that had served as the original factory was moved across the street. The senior Knechts, who had been living in it, found a home with extra land near Jersey and Pataskala, in Ohio, and were pleased to move to their new home.

Chapter 11

SOME INTERESTING PEOPLE AND EVENTS

AN ACCOUNTANT WE COULD COUNT ON
We were fortunate to have a top-notch accountant on our management staff. Bill Kirkwood joined us early in his career. He didn't have a college degree. He didn't need one. During his teenage years, he became fascinated with computers and their potential.

His father was an attorney, and perhaps Bill inherited a sharp mind. In any case, he came to work for us with a good sense of what a computer is capable of doing and soon demonstrated his skills for us. Later when we merged with Miles, and he was exposed to their sophisticated use of computer technology it made possible a quick adjustment to their management science.

When we had the opportunity to reacquire the business from Miles, Bill continued to show his thorough grasp of computer-generated financial data. I asked him for pro-forma financial statements reflecting the results of our expected operation of the business. In a short time he reported that operations during the first quarter of our take-over of the business, we would have a financial loss of approximately $250,000. However, in the first full year that followed, our operating profit would be double that amount. When I told him we must be sure his calculations were correct, he replied he had gone through the process three times and had come up with the same operating results each time. I reviewed his report to make sure our decision to proceed with reacquiring the business was comfortable, but I found no reason to question it. His forecasts proved to be accurate.

MORE NAME GAMES

Our fun with names didn't begin or end with identifying product. We had people with names that got attention.

One of the names that seemed unique for a company producing vegetarian foods that resembled meat was Joe Butcher, who worked for us as a foreman in production. Then there was Leslie Slaughter, who was often addressed by co-workers as "Less" Slaughter.

His responsibility was to provide quality assurance in the production of our foods. He lived in a house owned by our company. So it became habit for all of us to refer to the place where he lived as "The Slaughter House." Even after he and his wife purchased their own home, his first home continued to be called the "Slaughter House" or "The Former Slaughter House."

Worthington Foods, Inc. operating staff in 1983.
Seated from left to right: James C. Remer,
Dale E. Twomley, ARB, and Leslie R. Slaughter.
Standing from left to right: Evelyn A. Wiesner,
William T. Kirkwood, Richard S. Leiss, Craig F.
Newton, Nancy J. Minella, and Franklin D. Poston.

FEMALE ENGINEER DISTURBS US

In the early 1950s, our company was still using some equipment and methods with which it had begun business in 1939. There were reasons for the delay in becoming more efficient. One had to do with limited capital for investment in machines or technology.

Another was the continuing effect of wartime shortages. After the war, new food production equipment gradually became available. We also began to find more opportunities for financing our growth and modernizing operations.

The method used in fixing labels to cans and then packing the cans in cartons was one of the procedures that needed upgrading. Priscilla McNealy had been our most skilled employee in applying labels to cans of various products and packing them in cartons.

The process involved selecting a folded empty carton, opening it, adjusting the flaps, and finally stapling the bottom flaps with a foot powered stapling machine. The carton was then placed on a stand, open side up, and loaded by hand one can at a time until the carton was filled with twenty-four cans. As soon as the carton was full, the top flaps were glued with a hand held brush, and the carton then was placed upside down on a pallet made of wood to allow the glued flaps to dry. Each filled carton weighed about thirty-four pounds.

It's clear to see how Priscilla, or anyone else doing the job, could be very weary after a few hours of this kind of effort. For the most part, applying the labels to each can was somewhat mechanized. The labeling machine had a track down which cans simply rolled under gravitational force. A stack of printed labels was placed under the track, and as the cans rolled along each one received a drop of glue that caused the label to stick to the can. One end of the label received some glue as well, so the label not only stuck to the can, it also stuck to itself. It's obvious, labeling and packing canned foods was very labor intensive, and why we were ready to try equipment that offered any degree of automation.

By keeping an eye on advertisements appearing in food equipment magazines, we eventually saw a labeling and packaging machine that seemed to fit our needs. We ordered one and eagerly waited for it to arrive. The day came when I received a telephone call to notify me that the new machine had been delivered, together with information that an engineer also would come to assist in setting it up and to demonstrate how the machine is operated.

The next day the engineer arrived. I was a little surprised to see the engineer was female, blonde, and slender. She changed into coveralls and was ready for work. In the meantime our own engineers and a couple of male helpers had been alerted and were ready, tools in hand, to assist. There are times when being prepared, as well as being ready, to assist is important. They were not prepared, I observed, to have a blonde, female engineer, tell them, and more importantly, show them what needed to be done. They all had their tools with which to work, but all the men just seemed helpless. The blonde engineer alone seemed to know what to do.

They were not prepared, I observed, to have a blonde, female engineer, tell them, and more importantly, show them what needed to be done. They all had their tools with which to work, but all the men just seemed helpless.

In a couple of hours, she had the equipment set up and ready to try. By this time our own people were looking a bit embarrassed and glancing sheepishly at the tools in their hands. The visiting engineer called for some cans to be labeled and cartons to be packed.

The equipment worked even better than we had expected. The visiting engineer went to the women's locker room, changed into travel clothes, and was gone. We had taken a big step toward more efficient production, and Priscilla could be moved to a less strenuous job. In today's economy an episode such as this would hardly cause a ripple, but fifty or sixty years ago it provided a few laughs for us, and a story worth sharing.

ADDITIONAL ENGINEERS

As indicated earlier, B.J. Knecht was our official plan engineer until he retired after forty years of service. His natural skills had developed over years of work experience before and during employment with Worthington Foods. His practical knowledge was invaluable to us, and we were pleased to have him on our payroll until the date of his retirement.

We were fortunate in having his son, Bernath L. Knecht, and generally known as "BL," also working for us as an engineer with formal training and a degree. Whenever a problem or project needed further technical skills, we could turn to him for the help we needed. He was aided by an assistant, Sherri Babcock, who also had a degree in engineering. Together the two of them made a harmonious and strong team contributing effectively to new challenges and needs. All three were active members of our local Adventist Church and did much in meeting the needs there as well.

HELP FROM A MOVIE STAR

As stated elsewhere in this book, we marketed our products using a very low advertising budget. For us to spend more than $25,000 in one year was unusual.

So it was with some misgivings that we agreed with the company providing help with our advertising to use the services of Miss Ohio State. She came out to our place of business and posed for pictures as well as authorizing us to use her name.

We prepared a recipe booklet that had her photograph on the cover. In theory, at least, the recipes had her endorsement. After graduating from Ohio State University, she went to Hollywood and became a star. She became more famous when she married Howard Hughes. Her name was Jean Peters. We remember with pride and with gratitude the help she gave us. We're grateful, too, for the ideas and help of the Hoover advertising agency in arranging for her services.

> *She became more famous when she married Howard Hughes.*

FEMALE EMPLOYEES AT WORTHINGTON FOODS

Women working at Worthington Foods made significant and unique contributions to the growth and success of the company. Beth Mitchell, employed with Worthington Foods for twenty-two years, is one example. After starting as a part-time employee, she moved into a full-time position working with Sibyl Richards in accounting.

Her skills, including familiarity with products and inventory control, to which she had been exposed in her accounting experience, came to the attention of Tom Kimbrow and Harold Linsley, who were the sales manager and assistant sales manager at the time. When Daisy Patrick retired as secretary in sales management, Beth took her place.

Beth helped plan and conduct our annual marketing staff meetings, participated actively in trade shows where Worthington Foods displayed and sampled products, and traveled to camp meetings from New York to Oregon. Her help contributed to sales growth that generally resulted.

Beth says: "My career at Worthington Foods was a wonderful experience for me both professionally and personally. I cherish the wonderful friendships that I have been able to maintain over the years. It always felt like family." Beth continues to have an impact by keeping in touch with other former employees, who appreciate the connection.

Evelyn Wiesner is another woman who contributed to the success of Worthington Foods, and to my own accomplishments, for many years. Evelyn joined Worthington Foods in the mid-1950s as my secretary when I was general manager, and we made a good team. She was conscientious and careful, and all of us came to count on Evelyn. We missed her when she was away from the office following her passion for travel and visiting exotic destinations from Antarctica to Asia. Evelyn continued to work closely with me as I advanced from general manager to president to chairman of the board, taking on increasing responsibility as I did.

Evelyn moved to our accounting department after I retired, continuing there until her own retirement. Since retiring, she has continued to pursue her long-time interest in travel and frequently has new stories from far-away places to share with her former co-workers and friends.

DISASTER AVERTED

In going through records of the early history of the company I discovered a story that describes an incident that could have been fatal to a number of people. Fortunately, no deaths took place, but exposure to that possibility was dangerously close.

At the time, a written account was prepared by B.J. Knecht, our plant engineer and one of the employees who himself was involved in what happened. Because I had not yet joined the company, the story is based on his report.

As stated earlier, the company began as Special Foods. Storage, production, and administrative procedures were all conducted in a house that had been purchased for use as the first factory. A new boiler was installed in the basement under office space occupied by Bill Robinson who was managing the company at the time. For several days he had complained of headaches, but tried to ignore them. B.J. came to work one morning to prepare wheat gluten for use that day.

Later in the day, he remembered seeing one of the employees looking and acting in a strange way. He seemed to have a vacant stare and spoke with disconnected sentences. Another employee was standing at a window peering out but apparently not seeing much. At this point, B.J. himself felt faint and collapsed. He was taken out of the building where he quickly regained consciousness. By this time, all of the workers in the building were feeling faint, dizzy and sick. The problem was carbon monoxide from the new furnace, which was not working properly. Everyone was grateful the problem was discovered soon enough to prevent disaster.

A COMPLAINT TAKES AN UNEXPECTED TURN

Occasionally, we received a complaint from a customer, and I made it a policy to deal personally with all complaints regardless of their nature. My reasons for doing this were twofold. First, it made me fully aware of problems we might be having in our manufacturing or packaging processes. And second, it gave me an opportunity to reassure the customer that his or her complaint had come to the attention of top management in the company.

One day we received a letter from four female students at a university in Illinois. In reading the letter, it was clear to me that they were trying to include some humor in the message they were communicating. There was enough sarcasm in the way the letter was written to indicate this.

Their letter stated they had purchased a can of Choplets at a nearby store but later were disappointed in their purchase. The letter went on to say they had prepared the Choplets according to instructions on the can label, but none of them found the product to be what they had expected. They claimed they were not sure they had much stomach left after eating the Choplets, and to make matters worse, their pet dog refused to eat it. The letter ended with the signatures of all four of the young women,

In reply, I sent them a letter expressing regret at their disappointment and enclosed a check for $1.49, which is what they said they had paid for the Choplets. The check was made payable to all four of them. In my letter I went on to say we were sorry they didn't care for the product. However, we were pleased it might have helped reduce their stomachs because it was our understanding that many co-eds worked hard to reduce stomach size. I wrote further that I wasn't surprised their pet dog refused to eat it because it was human food not dog food. In closing, I thanked them for writing to express their complaint.

Several weeks went by without further word from them. We concluded the whole matter might be ended. Then a letter arrived in the mail together with a package. The letter was from the four students. The package contained a necktie with a hand-painted color image of a can of Choplets. The letter was addressed to "our favorite food company manager." They expressed pleasure over the exchange of correspondence and said they hoped the necktie would demonstrate their feelings. Which all goes to prove what Grandma said: "You can catch more flies with honey than you can with vinegar!"

Chapter 12

A FIRE AT THE FACTORY

In the year 1960, we had a fire in the starch-processing department of our plant that ultimately provided more humor than alarm. It began seriously enough and could have got out of hand, but the right people were there when they were needed. Most good stories need some background information to create a setting for the climax of the story. This tale is no exception to that principle.

We had two Harding family members on our board. They were brothers. and both were physicians. One was George T. Harding III, and the other was Warren G. Harding II. They were nephews of former President Warren Harding and were active in the Columbus medical community. George was the chief medical director at Harding Hospital and is recognized as the founder of our company. Warren was the administrator at Grant Hospital in Columbus.

Dr. Warren Harding was a skilled teller of stories and always seemed to have one to share at board meetings. I envied his skills and wished for the day when I might have a good story to tell at one of our meetings. The fire at our factory provided an opportunity.

The purpose of our starch processing was to provide cost

saving in disposing of starch washed out of flour to obtain the wheat gluten we needed for our food production. More starch than gluten created a challenge. Our response was to dry the starch on a heated drum dryer. A thin film of starch and water was allowed to form and then dry on the drum as it turned. After one revolution of the drum, a blade removed the dried starch and deposited it in flake form in a conveyor that took it to a hammer mill for pulverizing.

The starch powder was then blown upward into a cyclone chamber located just below the ceiling. After cooling the starch was returned to floor level where it was bagged, and later sold as wallpaper paste. Anyone familiar with wallpaper paste knows how slippery it can be when wet. In dry dust form, it is highly flammable. The entire starch processing operation was located in a one-story addition to the main plant. The addition had a rounded roof, often referred to as a barrel roof.

In the food manufacturing portion of our factory, we had a constant struggle cleaning floors and equipment after processing wheat gluten all day. Bernie discovered a way to cope with this problem when he learned a manufacturer of pumps had developed a high-pressure model that could be connected to an ordinary water line and increase pressure to almost 200 pounds. Users had to make sure the hose was not directed at other employees because the pressure was strong enough to tear off caps workers had on their heads or tools out of their hands.

One Sunday we found it necessary to run the drum dryer in an effort to catch up with an accumulation of starch. I was working in our yard when I had a telephone call from Elsie, Bernie's wife. (They lived in the house that had been our original plant and was located adjacent to the factory.)

"Allan," she said, "Better come to the factory right away. It's on fire!"

We lived just two blocks away from the plant. Looking in the direction of the factory, I could see a long column of black smoke rising into the air.

I was at the plant in a matter of minutes and found Bernie already there shutting down equipment that had been running. Somehow a spark had ignited the starch dust in the cyclone and a minor explosion had set it ablaze.

A Fire at the Factory

"Bernie!" I shouted. "Get the high-pressure pump and a hose. Maybe we can stop the fire before it gets out of hand!"

By now he was there, pump and hose in hand. Elsie, in the meantime, called the local fire department, which at that time was manned by volunteers. The fire department volunteers arrived at the same moment Bernie got to the scene with the high-pressure pump and hose. We could hear the men on the roof. They soon began chopping with their axes to get at the cyclone area where the fire had started. The explosion that accompanied the initial blast sent starch dust all over the roof.

Timing for what happened next couldn't have been planned better. Just as the volunteers were able to make the first opening in the roof and could peer down into the room, Bernie had water at 200 pounds pressure shooting up into the same area. The stream of water knocked off the helmets of the volunteer firemen, but worse yet, began to mix with the starch dust that had settled on the roof. The roof suddenly became more slippery than an ice slide.

The next sounds we heard were curses as the men began to lose their footing and slide down the barrel roof toward the eaves. In desperation they clung to the eave trough, but as they slid over the edge of the roof their jackets were pulled up over their heads and they could see nothing. Inside the building, looking out a window, we could see their boots dangling and heard shouts. I rushed out of the building and yelled, "Let go! You're only four feet off the ground!" Eventually, they did. In a few minutes, they picked themselves up, retrieved their helmets and axes, got in their truck, and drove off without any response to my words of appreciation for their help.

By this time the fire was totally under control and presented no further danger. Bernie restored

> *Just as the volunteers were able to make the first opening in the roof and could peer down into the room, Bernie had water at 200 pounds pressure shooting up into the same area. The stream of water knocked off the helmets of the volunteer firemen, but worse yet, began to mix with the starch dust that had settled on the roof. The roof suddenly became more slippery than an ice slide.*

order but left all equipment idle. I went to the office to call my wife, Mickey, to tell her everything was OK. While there I had a telephone call from a reporter for the *Columbus Dispatch*. He had called, he said, because he heard we had a fire and wanted to know how serious it was. I told him it had not been as bad as it could have been.

I said something like this to him, "The fire was pretty much confined to the cyclone, and didn't spread enough to be a serious threat."

There was a pause, then this response, "Cyclone? Did you have a cyclone, too?"

I tried to reassure him that I was talking about equipment, not the weather. But his next question suggested he either hadn't heard me or didn't understand. "How much will it cost to repair all the damage?"

My reply, "My guess is it won't run over a thousand dollars." No further calls were received, and no article appeared in the paper. I guess I didn't have a real news story, but I did have a story I could tell at our next board meeting.

Chapter 13

MERGER

During the late 1960s, a federally funded study of American eating habits was made. Much of the early research was conducted at Stanford University. Results were published showing a possible link between cholesterol levels in humans and the incidence of heart disease in people. Because the human body produces some cholesterol for its own needs, there were food scientists, Kelly, our own scientist being one, who were not so sure all the conclusions reached in the study were valid.

In spite of the questions raised by some food scientists, the published data was widely circulated in the food industry. Animal fats were identified as the real source of the problem. Because of the fat present in yolks, eggs were listed as serious contributors to high cholesterol levels. Ham and other meats were also named heavy sources. A cartoon published in a newspaper and later placed on billboards showed a hen and a pig having a conversation. The pig is quoted as saying, "You are lucky to be blamed for only a token contribution to the problem, but my entire body is condemned."

The published report created a real stir in the food industry. Food manufacturers began asking themselves, what's expected of us? What can we do? There were some who concluded they must find a way to provide satisfactory replacements for the traditional "ham and eggs." The problem, however, extended beyond breakfast fare.

By the time of the study, Worthington Foods had become the largest producer of vegetable protein foods in America, having demonstrated considerable experience and technology in making them. Companies with national and global reputations, seeing new potential, began making direct and indirect contact with us hinting at possible merger or acquisition. Among these were Beatrice Foods, Hershey Chocolates, Coca-Cola, Staleys, and others all with varying degrees of interest.

ARB in front of WFI facilities on Proprietors Road circa 1968-69.
Photo courtesy of Harding Heritage Foundation of Worthington.

At first, we resisted these advances, then began to recognize that most of the companies were already well established in the market, and could ultimately force their way into vegetable protein food production whether we liked it or not, simply because they had access to financial and research sources beyond our means. How can we make sure we survive? Finding the right partner, each using its own strength in serving its designated market seemed like the best answer.

Miles Laboratories with headquarters in Elkhart, Indiana, also contacted us just as we were about to make a choice. Dr. Walter Compton was president and CEO of Miles at the time. His vision was to develop products usable in place of eggs and meats high in fat content. He believed what we were doing at Worthington Foods was a step in the right direction but too limited. He proposed a merger under which Miles would focus its marketing efforts toward public institutions and consumers patronizing supermarket retail outlets. Worthington Foods, in turn, should continue serving private institutions and consumers purchasing products at health food and specialty stores.

Many American consumers were already familiar with "One A Day®" vitamins, "Alka-Seltzer®" and "S.O.S®" pads. This factor made the Miles offer attractive and we decided to accept it with a provision in the contract giving us the right to reacquire the business should Miles at any time decide it did not want to continue with the merger arrangement. The two companies merged in 1970 through an exchange of common stock.

At that time Worthington had annual sales of approximately ten million dollars, and it was agreed that the value of the business should be set at fifteen million. When final agreement was reached, the concept of merger was replaced by acquisition and Worthington Foods became a division of Miles Laboratories.

To meet its new sales objectives, Miles needed more production capacity than the Worthington Foods plant was able to provide. Management decided a larger factory was needed and initiated plans to rebuild with potential capacity at least four times greater. Construction was soon begun, and the new building was completed and ready for use in two years.

The new factory had features representing the latest thinking in food factory design, including tile floors for easy cleaning, air conditioning for clean air as well as for comfort, and interior painting providing a pleasing and relaxing atmosphere.

For efficiency and convenience in maintenance, the utility services were located on the second level of the building. Engineering and maintenance personnel occupied the third floor where space also was available for employee locker rooms and dining area.

Laboratories and a test kitchen for research, product development, and quality assurance were added in a building separate from the new factory but nearby for convenience.

Administrative office space was already in a separate building. Storage and shipping areas were also in a building nearby, separate from but connected to the main plant by conveyor systems.

A decision had already been made to have the Grocery Products Division of Miles provide marketing services for its new products. This division was located in Chicago. Miles also wanted to have additional production capacity at a factory site nearby.

This was important because further expansion at Worthington was impossible, there being no land available on which to build. Additional factory space was soon found in Schaumberg, Illinois, convenient for Miles' use.

Our affiliation with Miles brought important benefits to Worthington Foods. Dollar profits at Worthington may have been modest, but as new technology, new management systems, and new ways of thinking were absorbed, we began to experience more productivity and more efficiency in all phases of our business. In particular, a broader understanding of computers and more dependence on them added effectiveness to our way of doing things, whether it was research, marketing, or accounting.

As an example, a business plan forecasting units of sale by product and by months and years provided a way to determine when raw and packaging materials would be needed.

With this information, we were able to time our ordering so that delivery could be made as these materials were needed. As a result, we deferred expenses and saved storage space. Equally important, the business plan forecast of unit sales was used to determine production costs and margins of profit by product.

We were able to do this by asking our marketing people each year to forecast expected sales in terms of units of each product per month for three years in advance. Our sales manager and his helpers usually grumbled about this, claiming they were neither magicians nor prophets. Our management science people would then offer comfort by reminding them of opportunity to review and revise their numbers for years two and three after year one was ended. Marketing did not respond to this with enthusiasm but did find resulting product cost data helpful in establishing prices.

By using estimated costs of raw and packaging materials, based on historical data and adjusted for possible inflation, plus other direct and indirect expenses we were able to determine annual manufacturing costs, establish selling prices and arrive at margins of profit for each product. Monthly results, also obtained by computer, then showed any variance between forecasted and actual sales. This information was very valuable to effective management. Miles' knowledge and experience with these techniques made it possible to adapt the system to our Worthington business.

Although Miles headquarters was located in Elkhart, its grocery products division was in Chicago. John Grant was president and CEO of the division. I reported to him and learned a great deal from the experience. At our monthly meetings, we reviewed progress in relation to our business plan for the year. As part of this review, he would ask, "What risks do you see with the numbers you have used in your business plan, and what opportunities do you see in carrying out the plan for the coming year?" These questions helped us focus on what should be done to minimize risks and to maximize opportunities.

Following the merger, the Grocery Products Division initiated research at Worthington. The purpose of this was to develop a line of frozen foods designed for broad public consumption. The technology and manufacturing experience already in use by Worthington Foods provided results in a short time, and the Grocery Products Division was ready to begin sales. The brand name Morning Star Farms was chosen to identify the product line to clearly distinguish it from other products being sold.

Miles continued to push the sale of Morning Star Farms products with vigorous advertising and promotion. The annual sales volume reached fifteen million dollars, and the rate continued to grow as money devoted to advertising and promotion exceeded the dollar value of sales. For marketing its food products, Miles was using the same brokerage network they had retained for the sale of some of its other grocery products.

Because the new food items were frozen merchandise and the others were not, the marketing of the food items may have suffered a bit. Nevertheless, annual sales of the Morning Star Farms line were nearing a rate of twenty-five million dollars.

Chapter 14

WORK HARD—PLAY HARD

Before Mickey and I began living in Worthington, Jim Hagle and three associates were together one evening playing a card game called Rook. According to the story related to us after we became a part of the community, their game was interrupted by the sudden and unexpected arrival of the new pastor of the local church, who was making a few calls that evening to get better acquainted with some of his parishioners. Not knowing how he might feel about finding four of his congregation playing a card game, the men tried to conceal the evidence.

The pastor, detecting something was going on that the men were trying rather awkwardly to hide, nodded and made this casual comment, "I think there may be a skunk in the milk house."

From that date on, whenever a Saturday evening was open because their wives were having a little party of their own, and the men could get together for a game of Rook, it was a "skunk in the milk house" event.

Upon joining Special Foods in 1945, I was a little surprised to discover the company offices were located in a former bank building at 656 High Street. I was even more surprised to discover there were two regular sized bowling alleys located in the basement. Why there should be bowling alleys in a bank building raises interesting questions. This oddity didn't seem to disturb anyone connected with our company. On the contrary, it was accepted as a kind of bonus to be enjoyed by office workers and their families and friends. This seemed like a good attitude to take so I decided I should accept it too.

ARB outside the Special Foods office on High Street in downtown Worthington, Ohio. This former bank building included a bowling alley in the basement, which was a frequent site of after-hours fun.

The building was large enough to provide offices for Special Foods and extra space for rental to others. One of the other tenants was the Maple Lee Flower Shoppe. Those of us who didn't always remember birthdays and other anniversaries found the Shoppe convenient on those occasions when our memories failed us, and a last-minute purchase was necessary.

Now back to the bowling alleys for more details and the fun times we had there. These alleys were not in the same class with alleys available for public use today. They had conventional shiny hardwood lanes and official pins, but no automatic re-setting for pins.

We did this by hand for ourselves. There were no soft, reclining chairs with a nearby snack bar either. If we wanted refreshments, we provided them. Because this was a way to have inexpensive entertainment, Saturday nights often found us here with wives and friends who were happy to share in making refreshments available. The most frequent users of the bowling lanes were Jim Hagle, Al Buller, Ken Case, Lu Lyle, Ken Stepanske, and Kelly Hartman. Others would join us from time to time.

On the evening following the national election in the year 1952, we held a bowling party in our office alleys. Tom Dewey as the Republican candidate was considered by all news media the favorite to win by a large majority over Harry Truman, the

Democratic candidate. Dr. Charles Anderson, our company physician and a good friend as well, was with us that evening. He was a practicing psychiatrist at nearby Harding Hospital. After hearing the shocking news that Truman had won the election, Dr. Anderson declared in a solemn tone, "It's a sign of the end!" This struck the rest of us as being very funny. But after a good laugh, we all went home asking ourselves what the election results might mean for our country and for us as a company.

After several months of bowling together someone in our group suggested we explore the possibility of joining a local league. A number of teams made up of men from Worthington and Westerville had formed a league and were ready for expansion. They were genuinely pleased to have us join them. In a matter of weeks, they discovered that no one on our team smoked, used profanity, or relied on off-color jokes for humor. This often led to a discussion of our Adventist lifestyle and beliefs.

At times we were a little amused by their warning each other, in our presence, to avoid offending us by engaging in their customary habits. All of this became more meaningful when they saw we could not only bowl on the same level with them but were good enough at it to win the league championship title several times.

Bowling was a wintertime sport for us. When the weather was good, the golf course became inviting. There were days when we got up at dawn so we could play nine holes before getting to work. If that wasn't convenient or possible, there often was enough daylight after work hours for the nine holes missed in the morning. On Sundays, we could play eighteen holes with malted milks from the losers to the winners as a reward.

All of this might lead someone to ask if all we did was work and play. Our response to that question would be to point out the level of service in which most of our management people were engaged in their home conference or churches. Almost without exception, they were active members of conference committees and church boards, or served as church elders, Bible class teachers, or held other church leadership positions.

When bowling season was over, and the weather was unsuitable for golf, we could always play ping-pong. At the time we relocated our administrative offices from High Street to a former lumber company building on Proprietor's Road, we found some space in which we could set up a table for ping pong. Lunch periods and after-work hours found us competing in singles or doubles. Those of us who worked in the office were frequently joined by Kelly, who in spite of his artificial leg, showed he could compete with the best of us in either singles or doubles.

Jim and his wife Bobbie moved to Muirfield Village where he soon applied for membership in the club which owned and managed the golf course designed by Jack Nicklaus, the local golf hero who grew up in the area. The golf course had a policy limiting play to members only. Guests were allowed to play if accompanied by a member.

Jim's reputation as a golfer followed him to Muirfield where he was invited, from time to time, to play with a visiting guest. On one of these occasions, the course professional asked Jim if he was willing to play with the president of the Goodyear tire company who was in the area for a few days. The Goodyear blimp was actually on assignment to assist in photographing the golf tournament scheduled to begin a day or two later. Jim was pleased to play the role of golf host, for which the Goodyear president was so happy that he offered to take Jim for a ride in the blimp.

On a kind of spur of the moment in 1970, I submitted my name as an amateur interested in playing in a golf tournament sponsored jointly by the *Columbus Dispatch* newspaper and Children's Hospital for the benefit of the hospital. The tournament was to be held at the Columbus Country Club. At that time Arnold Palmer and Jack Nicklaus were considered the best golfers in America. Pro-am tournaments were popular and were held a day or two before the main P.G.A. event. I sent in my $300 entry fee and wondered who my playing partners, both professional and amateur would be.

In those days it was customary to place the names of amateurs in a container and draw them to determine which professional would be playing with them. The drawing was held on a Saturday with the names of participating players listed in the Sunday paper the following day. The game itself was scheduled for Tuesday. My feelings were somewhat mixed. Did I want to be paired with a well-known professional or would I be more comfortable playing with a lesser known pro?

Because Columbus is the hometown for Jack Nicklaus, local

interest in the tournament was high. To add further interest, Bob Hope, as a friend and admirer of Jack, had agreed to join Jack and his team of amateurs. The current and former governor of Ohio, James Rhodes, would also be present.

I was beginning to wonder if I had been wise in entering the tournament, but my name was in the "hat," so to speak, so there was nothing to do but wait and see how the drawing would go. Sunday morning I got up early, went to the front door, and picked up the newspaper. Quickly turning to the sports page, I was stunned when I read I was scheduled to play with Jack Nicklaus, Bob Hope, and two amateurs whose names I didn't recognize.

When I returned to the bedroom to share the news with my wife, Mickey's first words were, "Allan, what's wrong? You're white as a ghost!"

As I told her about my shock in discovering with whom I would be playing, she just smiled and said, "That's exciting news. You must be thrilled!"

> *Quickly turning to the sports page, I was stunned when I read I was scheduled to play with Jack Nicklaus, Bob Hope, and two amateurs whose names I didn't recognize.*

Soon friends were calling on the phone to ask if I'd seen the morning paper, and I suddenly realized I was getting more congratulations than sympathy.

Tournament playing time came. Former Lieutenant Governor Celeste was on the first tee to introduce Jack Nicklaus, Bob Hope, and the four nervous amateurs who would be playing with them.

At least 5,000 people were standing around the tee wanting to see Jack, and his friend, Bob Hope. Most of the crowd were pushing on the ropes surrounding us, eager to get autographs. We amateurs seemed to be in their way, so we also got pushed. Jack was very gracious about it all. He apologized to us amateurs saying he was sorry the crowd was acting so overeager.

After introductions, we all teed off. The pro golfers were expected to hit from the long tees. Jack hit his drive almost 300 yards. We amateurs hit from the tees normally used by club members. My drive traveled maybe as much as 40 yards, all on the ground. I felt I was fortunate even to hit my ball. I could have swung, missed, lost my balance, and fallen. (I've seen this happen when the golfer is trying too hard for a long drive).

As the match progressed, I got over some of my nervousness, but my voice sounded squeaky, due, I suppose, to the stress I was feeling. I managed to sink a putt for a birdie on hole No. 8. A few holes later I had another birdie, one stroke better than Jack who had a par. By this time I was feeling more confident and more comfortable.

Bob Hope continued to play with us. He had come not only to help his friend Jack but to enjoy a round of golf for himself. His final score for the day was in the low 80's—not bad for a man who was crowding 90 years of age.

On the 14th tee, he asked Jim Rhodes to pull their cart up to where I was about to hit my drive. He asked if I would be willing to take a suggestion, to which I, in my squeaky voice replied I would be pleased.

He then made this observation, "If you can shift a little more weight from the balls of your feet to your heels, I think you will hit your golf ball better. I tried his suggestion and hit a nice drive to the green where I sank my putt with one stroke.

Jack was standing on the green and exclaimed, "That's a four for a three!" meaning I had scored a real birdie to go along with the one-stroke handicap with which I was playing.

On the next hole, which was Number 15, I almost had a hole in one. I hit first among the amateurs. My drive landed on the par 3 green and rolled over the cup, stopping about thirty inches past the hole. I misjudged the return putt and could only salvage a par.

For the eighteen holes we played, our team had a combined score of eleven strokes under par, not enough to win, but respectable. My good friend and neighbor, Dr. George Harding IV, walked along with us taking photos, which I treasure and am proud to show friends who may, in fun, question whether I had really played with Jack and Bob.

The day proved to be the thrill of a lifetime.

Left to right: Bob Hope, Jack Nicklaus, two unidentified amateur golfers and ARB at a 1971 pro-am charity golf tournament in Columbus, Ohio.

Chapter 15

SPIN-OFF FROM MILES

The spin-off of Worthington Foods from Miles can best be understood if we first review the original merger agreement and how it was implemented. After a few weeks of negotiations in early 1970, the merger agreement was finalized. To make sure a future for Worthington Foods was guaranteed, two provisions were included in the agreement contract. The first was a joint commitment to continue the production and sale of products to the market, which Worthington had established. The second was a commitment on the part of Miles to give Worthington first option to buy back its business if Miles should, for any reason, decide to discontinue it.

Because Miles was primarily interested in serving the public market while the Worthington market was essentially limited to the health food trade and to Seventh-day Adventist outlets, the agreement for each organization to focus on its target market posed no problem. Worthington assisted Miles in the development of Scramblers, an egg replacement and a line of frozen vegetarian protein foods that were identified as meat analogs, the latter being marketed as Morning Star Farms products. Miles began the promotion and sale of these items as they became available. Investment in product introduction and sales promotion was necessarily a heavy expense, but it proved to be successful, and an annual sales volume of twenty-five million dollars was reached within a few years.

Worthington assisted Miles in the development of Scramblers, an egg replacement and a line of frozen vegetarian protein foods that were identified as meat analogs, the latter being marketed as Morning Star Farms products.

While Miles was directing its efforts toward developing a new market with new products, a large international company by the name of Bayer AG with headquarters and main plant in Germany was looking for a way to enter the U.S. market with its chemical and pharmaceutical products. Bayer was the company that earlier had developed and marketed Bayer aspirin. Miles was an attractive potential as a U.S. partner or subsidiary to Bayer AG. Business contacts and negotiation led to an acquisition agreement, and Miles became a part of the Bayer organization.

We were quite ignorant of details in the changes taking place within the Miles organization, but we believed that eventually someone would get in touch with us to let us know what the plans were for us. When no word had come after several months of waiting, we contacted Miles through its Grocery Products Division and asked if no visit meant no interest. We were told Bayer had no interest in the food business. When we asked further if this was an indication we could buy back the business, the answer was clear, "How much are you willing to offer?"

This prompt response caught us by surprise. We thought they might want a few weeks, or longer, to think about it. We said we were seriously interested but were not prepared to make an offer because there was important information we needed to help establish a value. Miles had invested in the construction of a new factory in Worthington and had spent money for product development as well as for promotion in introducing the new products into their market. We didn't know how many dollars it had taken to do all this, so could make no offer until we had some answers to these questions.

Their response to this was an even greater surprise to us. In summary, it was, "Our management consultants have just completed a survey. Here is a copy which may help you." With that comment I was handed a notebook a couple of inches thick. In it were recommendations on possible sale values for the Worthington business.

The first of three listed values was approximately twenty-one million dollars for an established on-going business. The second was a value of about fifteen million dollars based on the estimated cost of replacing plant and equipment. The third value of approximately nine million dollars was based on the possibility of a distress sale for lack of interest on the part of anyone in buying the business. I was encouraged to take the notebook with me back to Worthington where we could study it. Jim Hagle, Dr. George Harding IV, and I spent some hours in study and soul searching as we reviewed the contents. We concluded we should offer the lowest price that the consultants for Miles had suggested. It seemed like a good price at which to begin discussions. Miles could reject that offer if it was not acceptable, and we could consider other possibilities if we felt we wanted to pursue the matter further.

We made our offer of approximately nine million dollars and were surprised at the response, which was, "If we accept your offer, when will you be ready to close?" I hesitated for a moment and then explained it would take some time for us to raise the money needed. We don't know how long it will take to do that—maybe six months. After some discussion we agreed on a target date around the middle of October, and I returned to Worthington to discuss our next move with Jim and George. We were well aware of the burden that a buy-back would place on the three of us.

It was clear we needed a plan that would provide the funds required for a buy-out.

After considerable study and discussion, a plan began to take shape. We realized we would need to raise at least two million dollars through the sale of common stock. With this as a base, we felt we might be able to borrow the balance needed.

I made an appointment with the loan officer at the Huntington National Bank with whom we had done all of our banking business before the merger with Miles. He explained it was his opinion we were exploring a heavily leveraged buy-out and that four million dollars very likely was the maximum they, or any bank, could lend. That amount still left us about three and a half million short of our needs.

I made a point of keeping Miles-Bayer informed of our plans and progress or lack of it. In a few days, I had a call from John Grant, president of the Grocery Products Division, who said Miles was willing to advance the balance of funds needed if we would sign a promissory note to repay the money in four years. This was totally unexpected but a commitment that thrilled us.

Jim, George, and I agreed we must begin by raising the equity funds portion of our financing plan. We knew that finding prospective buyers would be a challenge. We visited former stockholders and new prospects in California, Florida, Tennessee, Maryland, and other states. We met with some success, but it was disappointing. By early summer I had an attaché case full of letters, lists of names of prospects, which we were trying to keep confidential which meant taking the attaché case with me wherever I went.

Jim, George, and I talked about raising the equity funds needed and agreed we had to decide how much common stock each of us would buy. It was time for me to have a serious talk with my wife about our personal financial position. We had recently made the final payment on our home mortgage. There was a modest amount of money in my retirement account with Miles, and I was within a few months of retirement age. In our conversation I told Mickey how sure I was that the business would be successful, but we couldn't move ahead unless Jim, George, and I each made a commitment to buy some of the stock we proposed to sell. I suggested we consider getting a new mortgage loan on our home, and that I draw all the money in my retirement account. These two sources would provide for about as much investment we could afford.

Mickey looked at me with unbelief in her eyes. I hastened to explain I believed this was the opportunity of a lifetime, and that I was sure it would be safe and ultimately rewarding.

After some further discussion, she said somewhat weakly, "When I married you, I guess I vowed it would be for better or for worse. This looks to me like the worst, but if you are sure you want to take the risk, I'll go along with you."

Jim, George, and I talked with former investors in our company, and with prospective investors about the opportunities facing a new revived Worthington Foods, we discovered it was more difficult to sell stock than we had anticipated. Some felt it

> "When I married you, I guess I vowed it would be for better or for worse. This looks to me like the worst, but if you are sure you want to take the risk, I'll go along with you."

was too risky. For others, the timing for investment was not right. One month before closing date we were still short about $500,000 in raising the necessary capital. There were some prospects still on our list to be contacted. We felt confident some of them would, in time, decide to make an investment, but we were short of our goal and forced to share the news with the bank, and with Miles.

The loan officer at the Huntington Bank with whom we had talked earlier about borrowing funds, said if we felt quite certain we could sell more stock, they were willing to loan $500,000 to Jim, George, and me on our personal signatures. We thanked him for this suggestion and asked for time to think about it.

After reviewing our plans for the buyout and further conversation with Miles management we decided to move ahead, with the middle of October as a tentative target date for closing the deal. Up to this point in time we had not discussed buyout plans with any of our employees at Worthington. To make sure we would have a workforce we held a meeting with our employee group and brought everyone up to date on what we were planning to do and why. We told the employees they had a choice of continuing at Worthington or accepting what other employment Miles had to offer. We then asked for their response and were surprised and greatly pleased to discover a one hundred per cent vote to continue with Worthington.

Worthington Foods, Inc. Board Officers following re-acquisition from Miles Laboratories, October 1982: George T. Harding IV, Vice-president and Secretary; James L. Hagle, Chairman and Treasurer; Allan R. Buller, President.

Chapter 16

STOLEN ATTACHE CASE

Negotiations for our buyout of the food business from Miles Laboratories went smoothly, but there was one event in the process that was near disastrous. It's a story in itself.

A number of details in our discussions needed review and agreement. An example was the use of brand names and labels. It could take some time for us at Worthington to design and print new labels. Would Miles be willing to allow us to continue using their labels, and if so, for how long? We arrived at a mutually satisfactory understanding on this issue, but there were more questions that needed discussion and agreement.

Each time we had a discussion, I made written notes of decisions or suggestions agreed upon and placed them in my attaché case. Because they were important and confidential, I kept the case with me at all times, taking it home with me in the evening and keeping it safe until morning when I returned to the office.

One August day seemed especially busy. At the end of the day, I felt exhausted, and the possibility of a swim at the nearby pool where our family had a membership seemed very inviting. I tossed the attaché case on the front seat of the car, locked the doors, and headed for the pool. It was still daylight, and I decided a quick dip was all I needed.

After a short swim, I returned to my car and immediately noticed the attaché was missing. A quick look at the car door on the driver's side showed evidence of tampering. I called the police at once. They were sympathetic, but not very encouraging.

"We have no doubts about break-in and robbery. The only problem is, the thief will probably just throw the case away when he discovers there is nothing in it of value he can use."

As he said this, the policeman held out a pad with a statement for me to sign indicating no dollar value could be given for the missing attaché. A minute later he was out of sight. It was getting dark, and I felt very much alone in my frustration.

As I lay awake that night, I tried to imagine what the thief might have done with the case that presumably had been discarded. The only picture that came to my mind was that of dumpsters I had seen in the area around the swimming pool. The next morning I was up with the sun and scrounging through dumpsters. By the time most people were going to work, I had gone through ten or twelve dumpsters in a futile search. I decided to give up further search. People seeing me go through the trash in dumpsters might think I was pilfering and call the police. The search did lead me to a couple of conclusions—the thief had not used a dumpster near the site of the theft, and people throw away a lot of strange stuff.

I went home for a shower. Being a firm believer in God's interest in our temporal needs, I prayed a silent prayer for help in finding the missing attaché. Then I went to the office to see if I could find a way to reconstruct what was lost. The possibilities did not appear encouraging.

About 2:30 in the afternoon, Evelyn, my secretary, called on our intercom and said, "There's a man on the phone who wants to talk to you."

"What's his name? Does he have any business connection?"

"He's not willing to give me his name or why he is calling. He says it's personal."

"OK, I'll take the call." Then after switching from intercom to telephone, I said, "Hello, this is Mr. Buller speaking."

A voice responds, "Mr. Buller, did you lose an attaché case?"

My heart stopped beating for a few seconds and then I responded, "Yes, why do you ask?"

"Well, I found one last night in the parking lot where I work in a restaurant close to the Continental Club swimming pool. When I looked inside, I found a business card with your name on it."

Silently I said, "Thank You, Lord!" Then out loud, "I'm glad to hear from you. How can we get together?"

> *Silently I said, "Thank You, Lord!"*

His reply, "I'll be working tonight. If you want to meet me in the parking lot, I'll be there at nine. By the way, my name is Howard."

At 8:45 I was at the parking lot wondering who and what I might discover. In a few minutes, a somewhat beat up car appeared, and a young man got out.

"Are you Howard?" I asked.

"Yes."

"I'm Allan Buller. I was glad to hear from you this afternoon."

"Let me open the trunk, and you can see what I found."

After I bent down to look it occurred to me this guy could have hit me on the head, thrown me in the trunk, and after that, who knows? But fortunately, it didn't go that way.

Instead, a feeling of relief swept over me, and I said, "There's no question. That's my attaché."

"You better look inside and see if everything is there."

I opened the case. It was filled with papers that looked very familiar. They weren't even very dirty! Then I turned to Howard. "This is great. Are you ready to return it to me now?"

"Yeah, I found the case on the ground outside the restaurant with papers scattered all around. I tried to gather everything up but don't know if I got it all."

It looked to me like everything was there. I reached into my pocket for my wallet and found two twenties. I handed them toward Howard, but he refused.

"Naw," he said. "That's OK. I'm glad you've got it all back."

I insisted, but he continued to refuse.

The next day I called his employer and told him what an honest and responsible dishwasher he had working for him. Then I told Nancy Minella, our human resource director the story and suggested I had found a good potential employee for our company.

A few days later Nancy dropped by my office and reported, "I don't think we want to hire this man. I've checked his employment record and find he has a police record and has served at least one sentence in jail."

"Sorry about that. I thought maybe he was a good prospect. But thanks for checking. Better put a hold on that employment offer."

A week or so went by, and then I received a telephone call. Again the calling party wouldn't give identification to Evelyn. I took the call.

A woman's voice says, "This is Howard's wife calling. Mr. Buller, Howard is in jail and wants to know if you are willing to bail him out. It will take $500 to pay his bail."

"Why is Howard in jail?" I ask.

"Well, he bought a radio from a friend. The police say it had been stolen, so they arrested him and locked him in jail."

"Sorry to hear that. I'll see if there is anything I can do."

After some thought I decided $500 was not too much to pay for getting my attaché case back. I took a check to the county jail and got Howard's release. Next, we went to join his wife. She was at home with their baby and some family members all looking a bit tearful. They thanked me profusely.

I left the home and family with this admonition, "Howard, I want to give you some advice if you'll accept it. Never buy a radio or anything else from someone on the street no matter how much of a bargain it is. Chances are it's stolen, and you'll only get into trouble if you buy it."

"Yes, Mr. Buller. Thank you, Mr. Buller."

"Goodbye, Howard, Mrs. Howard. Take good care of the baby."

I wonder what has become of Howard?

Chapter 17

SALES MEETINGS

WFI product labels typically emphasized that the contents contained no meat or animal products.
Photo courtesy of Harding Heritage Foundation of Worthington.

During its early years Special Foods held no sales meeting because it had no sales representatives. The demand for its products, particularly "Choplets" created by meat rationing during World War II, dropped dramatically when the war ended. Fortunately, the company had a sales base in the health food trade and in the Seventh-day Adventist market. But was this enough to keep the business alive and growing? Jim Hagle and I struggled with this question for some time, and ultimately concluded we must promote the use of our products through some form of advertising, and we must have someone to make sure retail sales outlets were stocking them.

The first salesman on our payroll was Bill Gersonde, who was living in St. Joseph, Michigan, after retiring as a flour salesman. Both Jim Hagle and I were acquainted with Bill, from both of us having lived in Berrien Springs, Michigan, just a few miles from Bill's home in St. Joe, and from having met him and his family in church from time to time. We weren't sure how Bill would fit in our marketing plans, which were pretty sketchy, because of our lack of experience in employing a salesman. Nor did we know how to proceed in broadening our market. We were quite sure Bill was not prepared to serve the health food trade, which seemed to be our primary market, and we didn't really need him for our Adventist market. We had no real experience or knowledge in how best to serve the public market, but it seemed to offer the best opportunity to use Bill's experience.

We hired him and set him to work calling on supermarkets and other retail food outlets. It was tough going. The public saw our products as an answer to a need during meat rationing, but when meat became available, interest in "Choplets" as a meat replacement no longer existed.

Bill was a product of "old school" salesmanship. By using a bit of high pressure, he was able to get a few stores to stock our products, but it didn't take long to see it was not taking us where we wanted to go. Bill saw this as clearly as we did and suggested he would like to make his retirement final. While we liked Bill and didn't want to release him, it seemed best for him and for us to let him go. We parted as good friends and continued to keep him informed on our progress.

After we had listed a sales job opening, we received an application from Lyman and Vickie Miller. Interviews led to our hiring both of them. I say both because it brought two people to our company who could strengthen our marketing program. Lyman was a salesman with experience, having served as a sales representative for a nationally known food company, and Vickie had conducted cooking classes and was prepared to do the same for us. She also had done taste-test sampling at retail stores, which is very helpful in introducing new products to consumers. There was opportunity for her to do this for us.

We now had the foundation for a sales force that could effectively serve the health food market and strengthen our efforts to reach individual Seventh-day Adventist and other consumers who were looking for new and better vegetarian foods. We felt we were now ready to hold our first sales meeting. A two-person sales force is hardly enough staff to justify a conference, but we scheduled one and included several of our strongest distributors whose service and experience were important to us. The event launched our practice of annual sales meetings held in Worthington one year and at other locations in alternate years.

One item that usually appeared on our agenda at sales meetings was a review of sales volume for each product in our line. We all recognized that not every item we began to make would survive in the market. Because our salesmen were in close contact with our customers, we found it helpful to get their input on which products were doing well and which were not. The weakness in this method was the difference in opinions among the sales representatives all of whom had customers with favorite products, determined to a large extent by culture or custom in their respective geographical regions. For example, customers in New England had a preference for products containing beans with a bland flavor, whereas customers in some of the southwestern states favored chili with a strong spicy flavor.

> *We all recognized that not every item we began to make would survive in the market.*

Our guideline for a product to be dropped was a volume of 5,000 units per year. On the surface this seemed reasonable enough, but it did make decisions difficult when they involved products with different appeal in different parts of the country.

One comment often heard during these discussions was, "Oh, no. Don't drop that one. That's a favorite with some of my best customers!"

As a consequence, it was with some hesitation that we brought the subject up at a sales meeting, but as difficult as it was we had to go through the process yearly or more often to maintain production efficiency and also product manufacturing cost.

These sales meetings did offer an opportunity for adding new products as well as deleting some. Kelly usually attended these meetings and would ask the salesmen for new product ideas based on their perception of what customers wanted. Their responses frequently led to the development of new items for which the retailer believed there would be a potential demand by their customers.

When we brought the salesmen together for our customary annual meeting, we had them all stay in the same hotel at night. We avoided nightly meetings with a planned agenda because we wanted the sales reps to have opportunities get together for their own "rap" sessions. This fostered a genuine camaraderie and encouraged the sharing of experiences. Sometimes they would begin their evening together by playing games and end it just talking.

At all times there were competitive efforts to share the best sales experience or a new joke. When the meetings were held at Worthington, all employees seemed to catch some of the spirit of the meeting, and the sale representatives were regarded somewhat as warriors going out to do battle on the front line, which in a sense they were. So the sales meetings usually had a positive and stimulating impact on all employees. This provided the benefit of feeling like a team.

As a part of the sales meeting plans, we usually included a banquet at which individual sales performance could be recognized and rewarded. When meetings were held locally, all employees were invited to further encourage team spirit. It was always an encouragement to us when someone said, "This was the best sales meeting we've ever had!" Or, "I wish the meeting was beginning tomorrow!"

When we began holding meetings at other locations than Worthington, we felt some concerns about benefits and success versus distractions. We discovered one way to assure good accommodations and good service was to contact major hotels that had recently opened for business and were wanting to test their readiness for groups and meetings larger than ours. We usually found them receptive to small conferences and often prepared to offer attractive rates.

Evelene Callahan was a part of our marketing staff for many years. She was the person at the home office who took calls from salesmen when they wanted to place telephone orders, convey instructions on shipments, or obtain information they needed and Harold Linsley, as assistant sales manager, relied on her for communications as did the salesmen.

Naturally, she was included in plans for the sales meetings. Her presence made sure she was kept informed of plans and instructions and added credibility to communications after the meetings. Evelene was blessed with a sense of humor that was contagious. She enjoyed talking with the sales reps and they in turn found it easy to talk with her.

At one of our meetings in Worthington she asked if anyone wanted to go out to get something to eat, and to see what the new outer belt around Columbus was like. Several of the men did, so she agreed to take them. They all got in one car and, of course, conversation with considerable bantering immediately began.

After they had been driving for some time and before anyone realized what was actually happening, they found themselves back at the hotel near the exit from which they had begun the trip. This meant they had made the entire circuit around Columbus. Even though the drive had been somewhat futile in that they had not stopped to eat, the men felt somewhat obligated to Evelene. They agreed among themselves that she should be compensated in some way for her time and effort. As she was getting out of the car with hotel guests standing nearby, they offered her several ten-dollar bills.

She could not resist the opportunity for a joke, so she rather loudly made this comment, "Is that all you guys are going to give me for the good time I've shown you?"

The men were a bit discomfited but the nearby hotel guests, as spectators of the whole scene, showed much interest and amusement.

Our company was blessed with people who were creative. Promoting vegetarian foods to the health food market and to health-minded consumers, looking for non-meat protein foods, including Seventh-day Adventists, took some effort. On the other hand, developing a broader market to include people who were accustomed to a diet that relied heavily on meat was a different story. High school and college-age consumers showed some interest based on the feeling it is morally unacceptable to kill animals for food or clothing. But older people whose eating habits were built around meats were more difficult to reach. We found cooking classes where preparation and taste testing could be done was one of the most effective ways to overcome habit or indifference.

Promoting vegetarian foods to the health food market and to health-minded consumers, looking for non-meat protein foods, including Seventh-day Adventists, took some effort.

As our marketing efforts progressed, we began to realize business was growing almost equally in three regions-the Atlantic coast states, the Midwest, and the Pacific coast. The importance of this resulted in decisions to open branch warehouses in each of these areas. The improved service we could offer customers and the economic benefits to us soon demonstrated the value of these moves.

Chapter 18

UNEXPECTED OPPORTUNITIES FOR ACQUISITIONS

Dr. Harry W. Miller was regarded by many as the "China Doctor." He was a Seventh-day Adventist missionary physician who served for decades in mainland China and later in Hong Kong. His humanitarian work attracted the attention of General and Madame Chiang Kai-shek. On a number of occasions, Dr. Miller provided medical services for them. In turn, they gave him encouragement and tangible help in establishing a hospital on the mainland and another one in Hong Kong.

Dr. Miller's skills were not limited to medical practice. He had a strong interest in nutrition and devoted some of his time to examining the relationship between diet and health. While serving in China, he noted the wide use of tofu, soybean sprouts, and whole soybeans in the diet of the Chinese people. He concluded soybeans offer nutritional value when used in the human diet.

When Dr. Miller retired as a missionary, he settled in Mount Vernon, Ohio. Even though he was an octogenarian in age, he was determined to pursue his interest in finding a way in which soy products could fill a role in providing better nutrition for people. One of his goals was to discover how to make milk from cooked soybeans, which, fortified with other nutrients for balance, could be used in place of cow's milk. He believed such a product could be used as an infant formula, and also as a replacement for cow's milk for older children and adults suffering from allergic reactions to animal milk.

His first step was to organize a company under the name International Nutrition Laboratories. This provided a professional front for the work he wanted to do. He was now ready to begin exploration of his dream to make soybean milk. He faced two obstacles that must be confronted: (1) an unpleasant flavor, which soybeans give to products in which they are used as an ingredient, (pressure from the food industry in time brought improvement) and (2) the attitude of people who believe soybeans are food for cattle and other livestock, not for human beings.

It was an uphill battle for Dr. Miller, but as a medical missionary, he was accustomed to struggling with problems. He continued with his experiments and market testing. Eventually, he was successful in making soybean milk that met nutritional standards for infant feeding, and began marketing the product under the brand name "Soyalac."

Not content with his success in producing a soymilk, he began experimenting with the development and production of vegetarian foods made from wheat gluten. This placed him in direct competition with Worthington Foods and other manufacturers of similar foods. By the mid-1940s, Miller's Cutlets and Miller's Cutlet Burger were being produced in the Mount Vernon plant. Although we were in competition with each other, we managed to maintain a friendly relationship with Dr. Miller.

From time to time we had the opportunity to meet and share ideas of mutual interest such as how we might create more public awareness of what we were doing in the field of vegetarian foods and how we might increase consumer demand for them. As he got older, Dr. Miller had less interest in managing a food manufacturing operation and became more interested in expanding his research activity. This led us both to a discussion of the possibility of merging our two companies. Out of these discussions, an agreement was reached for Worthington Foods to buy the rights to use the formulas, trade names, and manufacturing know-how in the manufacture and marketing of Miller's Cutlets and Cutlet Burger and for Loma Linda Foods to negotiate for the acquisition of rights to produce and market Soyalac.

Worthington Foods did not need the Miller plant in Mount Vernon because we had our own manufacturing facilities in Worthington. On the other hand, Loma Linda Foods needed a place to produce soymilk and was able to purchase the Mt. Vernon factory. These changes proved to be beneficial to all three companies.

Our acquisition of the Miller vegetarian food business took place in 1950. This was the first, but not the only merger or acquisition in which Worthington Foods was involved.

From my experience in working with him, I became quite intimately acquainted with Dr. Miller. At an age well into 80 years, he was mentally sharp and truly a man of vision. I felt it was a privilege to know him and I trust some of his knowledge of nutrition and his outlook on life in general rubbed off on me.

> At an age well into 80 years, he was mentally sharp and truly a man of vision.

In our contacts with Dr. Miller, we had the opportunity to meet and talk with his son, also named Harry. He seemed to be following in the footsteps of his father by active participation in food manufacturing and maintaining an interest in nutrition. Some years later he was helpful in our acquisition of the Madison Food Company. Dr. Miller decided to relocate to California, and he moved his International Nutrition Laboratories to that state and continued his research activities there.

About ten years after our acquisition of the Miller vegetarian food business, we received a call from George McKay who, with his father, was in the banking business in Battle Creek, Michigan. He suggested a visit at which we could discuss the future of the Battle Creek Food Company that he and his father had acquired after the death of Dr. Kellogg. This visit provided the opportunity to acquire the business of the Battle Creek Food Company. The McKays were willing to retain the factory in Battle Creek which simplified the deal for us.

The acquisition of the Battle Creek Food Company brought a number of real benefits to us. It created a favorable impression among customers in our existing market. We received rights to manufacture and market products very similar to those in our line. Perhaps of most importance, we received formulas and know-how to make new products compatible with some we were already making but not a duplication of them. Our total combined sales volume for the year exceeded one million dollars for the first time in our history.

The services of Josephine Williams, an experienced dietitian who had been with Battle Creek Food Company, were available until she was ready to retire. We found her help to be valuable in assisting us with formula identification and clarification. Four salesmen and several other key employees also joined us. We felt very fortunate to have an opportunity to acquire the Battle Creek Food Company. We asked George McKay to serve as a member of our board of directors. His knowledge of the Battle Creek Food Company business was helpful as we made adjustments to changes resulting from the acquisition.

Worthington Foods, Inc. Board circa 1960, following acquisition of the Battle Creek Food Co. Left to right: George McKay, Kelly Hartman, Warren Harding II, Jim Hagle, ARB, George Harding III, Harrison Evans.

Chapter 19

BULLER HALL

When we sold Worthington Foods to the W.K. Kellogg Co, shareholders who held stock in our company received a cash payment of twenty-three dollars per share. For some shareholders this represented a significant capital gain. During the years we had operated as a private corporation there had been quite a few stock splits and other actions that resulted in a per share cost of less than one dollar for many shareholders. I was fortunate to be one of them.

Out of the proceeds I received, I invested a substantial amount in an irrevocable annuity issued through the investment fund of the General Conference of Seventh-day Adventists. Provision was made for the annuity to be paid to Andrews University upon my death. At the same time, my wife Mickey and I as alumni, made an additional commitment to support student scholarships with annual contributions.

Dr. Niels-Erik Andreasen, president of Andrews, invited me to serve on a "Blue Ribbon" committee whose mission was to find a way to generate income for the school to minimize financial losses it was experiencing. The help this committee was able to provide led to the formation of a President's Council, most of whose members were business and professional people who were not employees of any organization operated by the Adventist church. I was invited to serve on this council. The council was able to make some suggestions that, together with cash contributions, proved to be helpful to the school.

Shortly after this, I was contacted by the university development officer who asked if I would be willing to make a lead gift toward the construction of an undergraduate student center. If this could be done, the building would be named in my honor. I was not sure I had adequate financial resources do this given the annuity I had already provided for the school and commitments I had made to help build a new church in the community where we lived. The maximum gift I said I felt I could make, seemed to satisfy the need, and I was informed Buller Hall would be built during the ensuing year. I believe this was a very gracious decision on the part of the school administration.

Dr. Andreasen's vision of a student center that would provide an environment to promote student-teacher interaction met the approval of the university board. A groundbreaking ceremony was held in April 2010, followed by construction of the building that included classrooms, teacher's offices, a student lounge, a 250-seat amphitheater, and a small chapel. As scheduled it was completed in time for dedication one year later. A ceremonial opening of the new building was conducted and full use initiated. As students and teaching staff began using the facilities, they seemed satisfied it provided all of the convenience and comfort promised.

I was able to visit the new building during the annual homecoming week, held shortly thereafter. I was impressed and pleased by the way in which everything seemed to be meeting the needs of students and faculty in the way Dr. Andreasen and his staff had expected.

Chapter 20
QUIZ TIME

The merger of Worthington Foods into Miles Laboratories created some confusion and some dismay on the part of Worthington customers, many of whom thought we were abandoning our mission of serving the Seventh-day Adventist and health food markets.

Letters from various parts of the U.S. began arriving with questions about the future of the business and our loyalty to the church. Some of these letters came directly to us, and others reached us through the Adventist Forum and its magazine, the *Spectrum*. It's important to address these because the answers will be helpful in explaining matters only partially addressed in other chapters of the book. There may be some repetition, but extra explanation is better than too little information.

QUESTION NO. 1:
What connection did Worthington Foods have with the Seventh-day Adventist Church?

As a private company and as a chartered corporation, Worthington Foods could have no direct connection with the Adventist Church, but individuals who were shareholders, employees, or members

> As a private company and as a chartered corporation, Worthington Foods could have no direct connection with the Adventist Church

of the board of directors could be, and were, members of Adventist churches nearest their homes. George T. Harding III, M.D., one of the principal founders of the company, was an Adventist, a graduate of Washington Missionary College (later Columbia Union College and now Washington Adventist University), and of the Loma Linda College of Medicine. Beginning in 1948 and continuing for several years he took a leave of absence from Harding Hospital in Worthington as its president and served as president of the College of Medical Evangelists of Loma Linda (now Loma Linda University).

James L. Hagle joined Worthington Foods (Special Foods at that time) as general manager. He, too, was an Adventist and a graduate of Emmanuel Missionary College (Andrews University). He was serving as president of Worthington Foods when it merged with Miles Laboratories in 1970. He was a member of the Ohio Conference of S.D.A. Executive Committee and the Columbia Union Conference S.D.A. Executive Committee. Later he was elected to serve on the Kettering Hospital Board.

For my part, I was an Adventist, a graduate of Emmanuel Missionary College (Andrews University) and of Ohio State University, where I obtained an M.B.A. During the more than fifty years I was employed at Worthington Foods, I served on the Ohio Conference of S.D.A. Executive Committee for 23 years and on the Columbia Union Conference of S.D.A. for 15 years.

Dale Twomley, an Adventist and alumnus of Andrews University, served as president from January 1986 until 1999, when he led negotiations for the sale of Worthington Foods to the Kellogg Company. He chaired the Andrews University business department before coming to Worthington. Dale has served in leadership roles at a variety of other Adventist academic institutions, including Shenandoah Valley Academy and Mount Vernon Academy. At the time of this writing, he is chairman of the Board of Directors of Fletcher Academy, an Adventist college preparatory school in western North Carolina.

George T. Harding IV, M.D. served as an officer and member of the board of directors of Worthington Foods for a number of years. He also is an Adventist and presently is a member of the faculty at Loma Linda University.

Most of our key employees at one time or another filled important offices in their local churches. From this, one can see a close working relationship with and support of the Adventist Church from people who were a key part of Worthington Foods throughout its history.

QUESTION NO. 2:
What were the important factors that led Worthington Foods into a merger agreement with Miles Laboratories?

We were not looking for a merger with another company at the time; however, a number of companies well established in the food business began to see us as a possible candidate for merger or acquisition. Their interest was aroused by federally funded research to determine if there was a possible correlation between a diet high in animal fats and the accumulation of cholesterol and plaque in human arteries. The research was done at Stanford University that confirmed the suspicion and released the report for public information.

Beef, chicken, pork, eggs, and other foods known to contain animal fats were all regarded as risk foods. Worthington Foods was known in the foods industry as a manufacturer of meat alternatives made without animal fat. It didn't require very much imagination to recognize that a national food company could quickly get into making foods without animal fat by acquiring a company already in the business.

Jim Hagle, as president of Worthington Foods, was contacted by a number of companies all of whom wanted to know if we were for sale. Among these were such firms as Hershey Chocolate, Beatrice Foods, and Coca-Cola.

Miles Laboratories was a latecomer in the pursuit of our business. At first, we were not

Jim Hagle, as president of Worthington Foods, was contacted by a number of companies all of whom wanted to know if we were for sale. Among these were such firms as Hershey Chocolate, Beatrice Foods, and Coca-Cola.

particularly interested, but the significance and urgency of the entire matter required prompt action. After talking with Dr. Walter Compton, the president of Miles, we discovered a willingness to see Worthington Foods continue serving the Adventist and health foods market while Miles focused on the public market. We thus began to see benefits in merging with their firm.

QUESTION NO. 3:
Did you, or do you, have any regrets about the acquisition of your company by Miles?

The arrangement we had with Miles called for an exchange of values that were important to both companies. We had knowledge and experience in the manufacture of vegetable protein foods. Miles had no knowledge of and no capability for manufacturing these foods. On the other hand, Miles had experience in the production and marketing of vitamins and several grocery store products such as window glass cleaner and insect repellent. Perhaps even more important Miles had a sophisticated business management style that went far beyond anything we had achieved.

Miles was eager to get into the production and marketing of vegetable protein foods, which they had decided to call "meat analogs." We were able to help them develop a line of products identified under the brand name "Morning Star Farms." These were formulated in the same way we produced them for our own market, with one exception.

Morning Star Farm products contained a higher level of flavoring to appeal to the typical consumer in the public market. Miles shared with us their management science experience and skills, which included not only financial management but also production planning and inventory control. It was with their help that we were able to establish sales projections, which enabled us to know in advance what could be expected in the way of production costs, and provide a basis for the ordering of materials to arrive at our plant when they were needed. We found it very helpful to know what margins of overhead and profit each product was projected to provide for the coming year.

QUESTION NO. 4:
Regaining ownership and control of your company brought products and a sales volume you were not expecting. What problems did this create for you and how did you resolve them?

Yes, there were some conditions that were new and unexpected. When we began negotiations for the return of our business, we were mentally prepared to resume the marketing of the Worthington line of foods that we had developed before the merger.

But, the total that eventually came with the purchase of the business included not only the Worthington brand, with which we were familiar, but also included all the food products that Miles had developed. This meant taking on the promotion and marketing of all Morning Star Farms meat analogs, the egg replacement product "Scramblers" and several less important items. The total dollar volume of annual sales had reached $25,000,000 by this time. Miles' new partner, Bayer AG, had no interest in retaining any of the food business in which Miles had become engaged.

A complicating factor was reliance by Miles on distributors and retailers who had no experience in the marketing of frozen foods. The vitamins, glass cleaner, insect repellent, and other items that Miles was producing were all non-frozen; therefore Miles had seen no need for using the channels of distribution and sales ordinarily relied upon by manufacturers of frozen foods They proposed we follow the same practice until we had the opportunity to explore the market more fully. We had not used the traditional channels for marketing frozen foods to public markets because our market was specialized and relatively small. To resolve the problem, we hired a man with experience in the marketing of frozen foods and made him our sales manager. It was a somewhat risky move, but we really didn't have any good alternative.

QUESTION NO. 5:
In 1992 Worthington Foods went public with its stock in an IPO. What were the circumstances that led the company to go public at this time, and were the results effective in accomplishing your objectives?

When we purchased the food business from Miles in 1982, we did not expect to get all that it had become; however, Bayer AG wanted to be totally free of any and all food manufacturing. Miles, therefore, encouraged us to take 100 percent of the total food production and marketing which included all Morning Star Farms products, the egg replacement Scramblers, and a few dried food items. It was a challenging opportunity, but we did not want to see the business go to some other company that might not have the same interest we felt. We agreed to take over the entire food operation, although we knew it would soon require more production capacity than our plant at Worthington could provide. It would be necessary to have more space, and very soon.

A local city ordinance was in effect which placed a limit on the square footage that could be constructed on the ten acres of land we owned at that time. Fortunately, we had seen this problem coming, sooner or later. Acting on what seemed to be inevitable, we had already explored the possibility of acquiring land in the city of Zanesville about sixty-five miles from Worthington. In an attempt to attract new business to its locality, Zanesville had created an industrial park and was willing to grant tax abatement and other incentives to a company bringing a manufacturing operation into the area. Under Dale Twomley's leadership, we purchased twelve acres of land and discovered we were the first new business in thirteen years to settle in the city limits.

Owning land is not enough to do any manufacturing. We hired an engineering firm that designed a facility with state of the art capacity for producing frozen foods.

Getting a new factory built as quickly as we needed one called for capital. Our current shareholders were willing to buy some stock, but it was not enough to meet our needs. An IPO (initial public offering) seemed to be the best answer. Accordingly, we applied for and received authorization to sell additional common stock. We hoped to place it on the market at $25.00 per share, but our stockbroker persuaded us that we had our sights too high and that $23.00 was more realistic. We took his recommendation and were able to sell enough to provide the money needed.

I was not directly involved in these transactions, although I was kept informed on the progress. Dale Twomley, as president, and Bill Kirkwood, as treasurer, handled the necessary details. After the stock was sold, stock market analysts, as is customary, were appointed to monitor the stock market and the price at which our stock was being traded. This was done for the benefit of shareholders. Their job was to evaluate the management of the business to make sure investors were getting value for their investment. This became somewhat of a problem for us. Naturally, the analysts and the investors were looking for maximum return. On the other hand, we felt it was important to keep our customers happy and to price merchandise for sale at levels that would be attractive to new customers. Also, we felt it was important to add, or modify, products that would also attract new customers. This placed the analysts and us in positions of conflict in policies.

> *We felt it was important to keep our customers happy and to price merchandise for sale at levels that would be attractive to new customers.*

Our management people spent a lot of time trying to resolve these issues, usually without success. In conclusion, I would say going public with our stock was more disappointing than rewarding.

Chapter 21

A SOLID FOUNDATION

I believe a foundation for any success, recognition, or honors I have received during my lifetime was laid during the years I spent in school at Emmanuel Missionary College, now operating as Andrews University, in Berrien Springs, Michigan. In making this point, I refer to more than classroom or academic activity. It was during the years I spent on campus that I was baptized and became a member of the Seventh-day Adventist Church. It was also during those years I met my future wife. Both of these experiences helped to stabilize my life and establish some personal goals.

I worked in the business office of the college and earned the dollars needed to cover tuition, books, and other school expenses. My father was employed in the engineering and maintenance department of the school. I lived at home within walking distance of the campus. Working to earn enough to cover education expenses gave me a sense of self-reliance that proved to be helpful in later years.

A student by the name of Mildred Walberg also worked in the business office as secretary for the business manager of the college. We developed a friendship that has lasted a lifetime. In those days it was generally expected that students might meet future marriage partners while attending school. In fact, it was not uncommon to see multiple weddings take place at the close of the school year. Although we first met while attending college and became engaged, we didn't actually get married until after our graduation, and I was in uniform as a U.S. Army non-commissioned officer.

But I don't want to get too far ahead of what I feel is important with respect to some of our school experiences. Both of us got deeply involved in extracurricular activities. Among other duties, I served as vice-president of the student body and later as president. I also was elected president of our senior class and served on a number of committees. Mildred (or "Mickey," a name she preferred) also served a year as vice-president of the student body during which she was responsible for planning student social events. She also was active in several other student activities and committees. We were both involved in music as well. She sang in the girls' choir, and I played bass saxophone in the college band.

The extracurricular activities in which we both were involved demanded considerable creative thinking and planning which was a help to both of us in later years. However, unstable conditions in the international arena and the imminence of war occupied our thinking to a larger degree than did a choice of careers at the time. We didn't spend much time considering whether this was good or bad. It was just a matter of adapting to reality.

Receiving an undergraduate diploma did not end my academic life. After I joined Worthington Foods, I attended graduate school and received an M.B.A. degree. In the year 2010, I was named an Andrews University alumnus of the year and was invited by Dr. Andreasen to attend commencement exercises for that year's graduating class. At this event I was granted an honorary degree as a Doctor of Humane Letters. While the other honorees and I were seated on the platform, the president presented diplomas to each member of the senior class.

During this part of the ceremony, we witnessed a surprising and romantic episode. One of the first to receive her diploma was a young woman. When her name was called, a man rose from his seat in the audience and made his way to the platform.

> To say that the relationship which Mickey and I enjoyed, and our later marriage, played an important part in my successes and the various honors I have since received is really an understatement

He kneeled in front of her and made a marriage proposal. Although a little flustered by the sudden and surprising turn of events, she must have accepted the proposal. We saw her nod her head and he returned to his seat. She accepted her diploma with another reason to be starry-eyed. I trust they both lived happily ever after!

To say that the relationship which Mickey and I enjoyed, and our later marriage, played an important part in my successes and the various honors I have since received is really an understatement. Without her support and encouragement, I could not have accomplished what I have been fortunate in achieving. It adds further meaning to my feeling that my experience at Andrews University gave me a strong foundation for later life.

In 1992, Allan and Mickey celebrated their 50th wedding anniversary in Maui. They were married for more than 70 years, from September 1942 until his death in March 2013 at age 95.

TEACH Services, Inc.
P U B L I S H I N G

We invite you to view the complete
selection of titles we publish at:
www.TEACHServices.com

We encourage you to write us
with your thoughts about this,
or any other book we publish at:
info@TEACHServices.com

TEACH Services' titles may be purchased in
bulk quantities for educational, fund-raising,
business, or promotional use.
bulksales@TEACHServices.com

Finally, if you are interested in seeing
your own book in print, please contact us at:
publishing@TEACHServices.com
We are happy to review your manuscript at no charge.

www.ingramcontent.com/pod-product-compliance
Lightning Source LLC
Chambersburg PA
CBHW070544170426
43200CB00011B/2541